Contents

Census 2001 Population Report

Mid-Year Population Estimates

Maps

Introduction

This publication is the first report from the 2001 Census of Population for Northern Ireland. It provides counts of the resident population, disaggregated by age and sex, for Northern Ireland and the 26 Local Government Districts. The population counts are also presented at Health and Social Services Board, Education and Library Board and NUTS Level III (European Union Nomenclature of Units for Territorial Statistics).

This report is produced in accordance with the provisions of the Census Act (Northern Ireland) 1969. As a statutory report it therefore relates only to the conduct of the Census in Northern Ireland. To assist the Northern Ireland Assembly in placing Northern Ireland Census figures in a wider context, it also includes some summary statistics on England, Scotland, Wales and the United Kingdom as a whole. This information is drawn from the reports laid before the Westminster Parliament and the Scottish Parliament in accordance with the statutory provisions of those administrations. The Censuses in England and Wales and in Scotland are the responsibilities of the Registrars General for England and Wales and Scotland, respectively.

Northern Ireland mid-year population estimates for 2001 are also included in this report. These estimates have been based on the results of the 2001 Census, adjusted to take account of births, deaths and migration between Census Day, 29 April 2001, and the mid-year date of 30 June 2001.

These results will be followed by a Key Statistics Report which will provide basic analysis of each of the Census questions, to be followed by Standard Tables and Census Area Statistics which provide more detailed crosstabular Census output. A timetable for the release of these results is included in the Census Output Prospectus which can be obtained on request from Census Customer Services or from the NISRA website at www.nisra.gov.uk.

As with all Census outputs, this report was made possible by the co-operation of members of the public in responding to the Census; the commitment of the Census field staff in delivering and collecting forms; and the assistance of many other people and organisations throughout all aspects of the Census. The Registrar General would like to thank all those who have contributed to this work.

Conduct of the Census

Results from the 2001 Census relate to Census Day, 29 April 2001. The Census placed a legal obligation on every household in which someone was usually resident on Census Day, and on every person who was a usual resident of a communal establishment, to complete a Census form. These forms were returned by post or collected by a Census Enumerator.

The Census was followed by a Census Coverage Survey (CCS), an independent count of people in a sample of small areas throughout Northern Ireland. The results of the CCS were combined with the data collected from the Census in order to allow estimates of households and people missed by the Census to be made. The figures presented here, as with all forthcoming reports on the 2001 Census, have been adjusted to allow for under-enumeration.

Population Base

The tables in this report relate to the usually resident population on Census Day. Students are recorded at their term-time address. In contrast to the 1991 Census, information on visitors has not been collected.

1

Tables and Geography

This report contains seven tables of Census Day information. Table 1 provides counts for males and females by single year of age for Northern Ireland as a whole. Table 2 provides corresponding counts for each Local Government District, while Tables 3-5 provide similar counts for Health and Social Services Boards, Education and Library Boards and NUTS Level III areas. Tables 6 and 7 provide information on the United Kingdom population. A set of tables of mid-year population estimates is also provided.

Mid-Year Population Estimates

Population counts have been the primary output from each Census of Population in Northern Ireland since 1926. Intercensal estimates have always been (and continue to be) based upon results from the preceding Census. The methodology employed for calculating the mid-year population estimates is based upon monitoring components of change over time – births, deaths, migration and other changes. The natural change component (births minus deaths) is known accurately in respect of every Local Government District from civil registration sources. The net migration component is currently based primarily on information from registrations with General Practitioners, as recorded by the Central Services Agency.

The usually resident population recorded in the 2001 Census is the starting point for the 2001 mid-year population estimates. This is rolled forward from Census Day (29 April) to the mid-year date (30 June) by ageing the population by 2 months, adding on the births, subtracting the deaths and adjusting for migration and other changes occurring during that period. The population counts from the Census and the mid-year population estimates are reported on the same basis with the exception of some small technical adjustments to the count of HM Forces.

Comparability with 1991

The Census is designed to provide the most accurate possible picture of the population on the day the Census is taken. Comparisons of the results contained in this report with counts from the 1991 Census will be affected by changes in the Local Government District boundaries, changes in definitions, and adjustment for under-enumeration in the 2001 Census figures. Whilst the effect of these changes is likely to be small relative to the population being measured, users interested in population changes are advised to use the mid-year population estimates, which are designed to measure such changes.

Confidentiality

The Registrar General has taken steps to ensure that the confidentiality of respondents is fully protected. All published results from the Census have been subject to a statistical process to ensure that individuals cannot be identified. This process may mean that population numbers in larger areas may not be equal to the sum of the populations in constituent smaller areas; any difference between the two figures will be very small.

September 2002

Further Information

More detailed results from the 2001 Census
will be published over the coming months.
These will include results for the range
of Census topics and for smaller areas;
supporting information on the Census
including definitions of Census terms;
statistics on the coverage of the Census;
and evaluation of the conduct of the Census.
Further information is available from the
Northern Ireland Statistics and Research
Agency website www.nisra.gov.uk and
Census Customer Services:

Census Customer Services
McAuley House
2-14 Castle Street
Belfast
BT1 1SA

Telephone: 028 90348160
Fax: 028 90348161
e-mail: census.nisra@dfpni.gov.uk

Copyright and reproduction of material from this report

This report (excluding agency logos) may
be reproduced free of charge in any format
or medium for research, private study or for
internal circulation within an organisation. This
is subject to it being reproduced accurately
and not used in a misleading context. The
material must be acknowledged as Crown
Copyright and the title of the report specified.
This report can also be accessed at the
Northern Ireland Statistics and Research
Agency website www.nisra.gov.uk. For any
other use of this material please apply for a
Click-Use Licence on the HMSO website at
http://www.hmso.gov.uk/click-use-home.htm,
or by writing to HMSO at

The Licensing Division
St Clements House
2-16 Colegate
Norwich
NR3 1BQ

Fax: +44 (0)1603 723000
e-mail: hmsolicensing@cabinet-office.x.gsi.gov.uk

Census 2001 Population Report

Table P1

Population at Census Day 2001: Resident population by single year of age and sex

Age	All Persons	Males	Females	Age	All Persons	Males	Females
All ages	1685267	821449	863818	50-54	98426	48484	49942
				50	19474	9765	9709
0-4	115238	59213	56025	51	19697	9721	9976
0	21683	11116	10567	52	19549	9641	9908
1	22363	11550	10813	53	19653	9578	10075
2	23264	11887	11377	54	20053	9779	10274
3	23584	12197	11387				
4	24344	12463	11881	55-59	88732	43585	45147
				55	18122	9025	9097
5-9	123050	63147	59903	56	18161	8873	9288
5	23883	12421	11462	57	18427	9081	9346
6	24064	12380	11684	58	18015	8783	9232
7	24400	12370	12030	59	16007	7823	8184
8	24907	12676	12231				
9	25796	13300	12496	60-64	73587	35401	38186
				60	14781	7189	7592
10-14	132664	68014	64650	61	14821	7153	7668
10	26189	13436	12753	62	14999	7178	7821
11	25963	13271	12692	63	14386	6963	7423
12	26403	13561	12842	64	14600	6918	7682
13	26997	13789	13208				
14	27112	13957	13155	65-69	65341	30406	34935
				65	13876	6554	7322
15-19	129201	65598	63603	66	13199	6269	6930
15	27104	13887	13217	67	12929	6011	6918
16	27182	13857	13325	68	12790	5784	7006
17	26276	13303	12973	69	12547	5788	6759
18	25392	12998	12394				
19	23247	11553	11694	70-74	57852	25069	32783
				70	12477	5490	6987
20-24	109385	54913	54472	71	11999	5275	6724
20	22791	11648	11143	72	11415	4964	6451
21	22449	11478	10971	73	10938	4618	6320
22	21717	10785	10932	74	11023	4722	6301
23	21166	10442	10724				
24	21262	10560	10702	75-79	46542	18562	27980
				75	10486	4317	6169
25-29	114704	56628	58076	76	9761	4058	5703
25	21621	10799	10822	77	9245	3712	5533
26	21684	10655	11029	78	8723	3324	5399
27	22933	11366	11567	79	8327	3151	5176
28	24021	11794	12227				
29	24445	12014	12431	80-84	30289	11090	19199
				80	7893	3036	4857
30-34	127517	62487	65030	81	7298	2743	4555
30	25275	12421	12854	82	5821	2157	3664
31	24965	12257	12708	83	4820	1647	3173
32	25532	12425	13107	84	4457	1507	2950
33	25781	12657	13124				
34	25964	12727	13237	85-89	16116	4707	11409
				85	4086	1270	2816
35-39	129639	63430	66209	86	3786	1140	2646
35	26120	12887	13233	87	3248	952	2296
36	26845	13119	13726	88	2790	789	2001
37	26198	12820	13378	89	2206	556	1650
38	25578	12591	12987				
39	24898	12013	12885	90 and over	7185	1597	5588
40-44	117335	57432	59903	Under 16	398056	204261	193795
40	24847	12209	12638				
41	24074	11774	12300	Under 18	451514	231421	220093
42	23039	11231	11808				
43	23217	11353	11864	16-44	700677	346601	354076
44	22158	10865	11293				
				45-59/64*	325023	179156	145867
45-49	102464	51686	50778				
45	21720	10895	10825	60/65** and over	261511	91431	170080
46	20582	10494	10088				
47	20513	10434	10079				
48	20298	10179	10119				
49	19351	9684	9667				

*   45 – 64 for males; 45 – 59 for females.

** 65 and over for males; 60 and over for females.

Table P2

Population at Census Day 2001: Resident population by single year of age and sex

Age	All Persons	Males	Females
All ages	48366	24242	24124
0-4	3575	1818	1757
0	677	350	327
1	724	381	343
2	745	378	367
3	693	336	357
4	736	373	363
5-9	3657	1865	1792
5	753	398	355
6	710	352	358
7	761	392	369
8	727	381	346
9	706	342	364
10-14	3636	1870	1766
10	739	388	351
11	718	352	366
12	678	345	333
13	770	396	374
14	731	389	342
15-19	3368	1745	1623
15	713	366	347
16	697	357	340
17	661	340	321
18	694	352	342
19	603	330	273
20-24	3100	1644	1456
20	611	342	269
21	659	310	349
22	619	346	273
23	594	320	274
24	617	326	291
25-29	3713	1941	1772
25	668	343	325
26	700	364	336
27	753	412	341
28	736	373	363
29	856	449	407
30-34	4229	2148	2081
30	838	422	416
31	854	433	421
32	862	447	415
33	844	420	424
34	831	426	405
35-39	4050	2068	1982
35	844	444	400
36	864	428	436
37	855	439	416
38	811	418	393
39	676	339	337
40-44	3289	1663	1626
40	692	346	346
41	673	341	332
42	641	328	313
43	644	315	329
44	639	333	306
45-49	2955	1486	1469
45	619	303	316
46	627	334	293
47	550	284	266
48	580	278	302
49	579	287	292
50-54	2954	1494	1460
50	575	295	280
51	590	288	302
52	582	314	268
53	574	281	293
54	633	316	317
55-59	2691	1314	1377
55	533	260	273
56	529	251	278
57	547	272	275
58	568	292	276
59	514	239	275
60-64	2029	986	1043
60	440	193	247
61	405	186	219
62	406	198	208
63	394	212	182
64	384	197	187
65-69	1612	782	830
65	342	177	165
66	350	163	187
67	298	145	153
68	309	143	166
69	313	154	159
70-74	1302	603	699
70	309	155	154
71	270	120	150
72	240	114	126
73	239	103	136
74	244	111	133
75-79	1000	411	589
75	207	86	121
76	232	103	129
77	181	78	103
78	203	82	121
79	177	62	115
80-84	678	256	422
80	172	70	102
81	161	52	109
82	148	62	86
83	113	44	69
84	84	28	56
85-89	354	97	257
85	94	26	68
86	87	22	65
87	65	17	48
88	56	19	37
89	52	13	39
90 and over	174	51	123
Under 16	11581	5919	5662
Under 18	12939	6616	6323
16-44	21036	10843	10193
45-59/64*	9586	5280	4306
60/65** and over	6163	2200	3963

*   45 – 64 for males; 45 – 59 for females.
**   65 and over for males; 60 and over for females.

8

Table P2

Population at Census Day 2001: Resident population by single year of age and sex

Age	All Persons	Males	Females		Age	All Persons	Males	Females
All ages	73244	35759	37485		50-54	5193	2544	2649
					50	941	477	464
0-4	4646	2406	2240		51	1036	481	555
0	816	420	396		52	1027	501	526
1	938	470	468		53	1116	553	563
2	973	504	469		54	1073	532	541
3	961	505	456					
4	958	507	451		55-59	4728	2388	2340
					55	996	503	493
5-9	4793	2459	2334		56	976	493	483
5	939	482	457		57	949	483	466
6	945	478	467		58	960	470	490
7	931	490	441		59	847	439	408
8	983	490	493					
9	995	519	476		60-64	3436	1662	1774
					60	692	334	358
10-14	5120	2660	2460		61	678	320	358
10	1013	518	495		62	719	342	377
11	1008	530	478		63	682	326	356
12	1046	539	507		64	665	340	325
13	1053	549	504					
14	1000	524	476		65-69	2891	1368	1523
					65	605	296	309
15-19	4860	2478	2382		66	610	311	299
15	1034	505	529		67	565	276	289
16	1050	538	512		68	571	245	326
17	1000	512	488		69	540	240	300
18	1003	513	490					
19	773	410	363		70-74	2618	1132	1486
					70	554	236	318
20-24	4075	2011	2064		71	534	223	311
20	869	433	436		72	512	226	286
21	811	433	378		73	519	240	279
22	785	372	413		74	499	207	292
23	827	413	414					
24	783	360	423		75-79	2091	873	1218
					75	482	195	287
25-29	4614	2332	2282		76	428	186	242
25	871	452	419		77	392	183	209
26	822	417	405		78	395	160	235
27	950	483	467		79	394	149	245
28	960	451	509					
29	1011	529	482		80-84	1542	590	952
					80	389	150	239
30-34	5558	2712	2846		81	375	133	242
30	1056	490	566		82	277	109	168
31	1015	491	524		83	268	114	154
32	1132	588	544		84	233	84	149
33	1199	586	613					
34	1156	557	599		85-89	775	234	541
					85	180	58	122
35-39	5744	2765	2979		86	203	59	144
35	1138	579	559		87	155	56	99
36	1209	594	615		88	141	39	102
37	1096	517	579		89	96	22	74
38	1172	579	593					
39	1129	496	633		90 and over	365	89	276
40-44	5405	2679	2726		Under 16	15593	8030	7563
40	1147	575	572					
41	1123	549	574		Under 18	17643	9080	8563
42	1041	509	532					
43	1106	537	569		16-44	29222	14472	14750
44	988	509	479					
					45-59/64*	16373	8971	7402
45-49	4790	2377	2413					
45	979	501	478		60/65** and over	12056	4286	7770
46	953	468	485					
47	943	467	476					
48	966	487	479					
49	949	454	495					

*   45 – 64 for males; 45 – 59 for females.
** 65 and over for males; 60 and over for females.

Table P2

Population at Census Day 2001: Resident population by single year of age and sex

Age	All Persons	Males	Females
All ages	54263	26923	27340
0-4	3971	1995	1976
0	723	366	357
1	861	387	474
2	804	420	384
3	806	423	383
4	777	399	378
5-9	4154	2135	2019
5	809	422	387
6	825	423	402
7	813	400	413
8	815	412	403
9	892	478	414
10-14	4549	2345	2204
10	879	432	447
11	888	462	426
12	911	482	429
13	925	482	443
14	946	487	459
15-19	4367	2224	2143
15	928	472	456
16	1035	520	515
17	898	451	447
18	865	449	416
19	641	332	309
20-24	3450	1824	1626
20	685	381	304
21	656	357	299
22	688	355	333
23	710	351	359
24	711	380	331
25-29	3763	1817	1946
25	693	348	345
26	661	336	325
27	779	403	376
28	775	369	406
29	855	361	494
30-34	3893	1977	1916
30	771	380	391
31	779	424	355
32	792	397	395
33	780	411	369
34	771	365	406
35-39	4047	2047	2000
35	768	403	365
36	852	429	423
37	835	424	411
38	798	398	400
39	794	393	401
40-44	3774	1952	1822
40	793	407	386
41	794	391	403
42	725	370	355
43	772	414	358
44	690	370	320
45-49	3265	1695	1570
45	697	361	336
46	645	331	314
47	638	314	324
48	695	391	304
49	590	298	292

Age	All Persons	Males	Females
50-54	3231	1600	1631
50	625	314	311
51	651	325	326
52	652	330	322
53	650	309	341
54	653	322	331
55-59	2815	1418	1397
55	595	304	291
56	580	287	293
57	564	271	293
58	549	287	262
59	527	269	258
60-64	2336	1146	1190
60	471	237	234
61	484	235	249
62	484	230	254
63	446	230	216
64	451	214	237
65-69	1981	946	1035
65	430	205	225
66	403	194	209
67	414	195	219
68	367	164	203
69	367	188	179
70-74	1758	740	1018
70	372	152	220
71	389	167	222
72	351	151	200
73	356	144	212
74	290	126	164
75-79	1397	560	837
75	336	136	200
76	288	112	176
77	280	114	166
78	261	110	151
79	232	88	144
80-84	879	320	559
80	228	89	139
81	203	70	133
82	197	70	127
83	125	55	70
84	126	36	90
85-89	448	133	315
85	113	37	76
86	113	40	73
87	88	24	64
88	76	20	56
89	58	12	46
90 and over	185	49	136
Under 16	13602	6947	6655
Under 18	15535	7918	7617
16-44	22366	11369	10997
45-59/64*	10457	5859	4598
60/65** and over	7838	2748	5090

*   45 – 64 for males; 45 – 59 for females.
** 65 and over for males; 60 and over for females.

Table P2

Population at Census Day 2001: Resident population by single year of age and sex

Age	All Persons	Males	Females
All ages	58610	28571	30039
0-4	3730	1877	1853
0	716	381	335
1	735	374	361
2	737	369	368
3	754	377	377
4	788	376	412
5-9	3969	2061	1908
5	740	361	379
6	790	404	386
7	801	415	386
8	804	418	386
9	834	463	371
10-14	4310	2210	2100
10	787	405	382
11	821	422	399
12	860	450	410
13	931	458	473
14	911	475	436
15-19	4112	2109	2003
15	875	462	413
16	884	468	416
17	877	433	444
18	856	436	420
19	620	310	310
20-24	3368	1707	1661
20	709	397	312
21	640	332	308
22	704	340	364
23	653	322	331
24	662	316	346
25-29	3765	1876	1889
25	672	329	343
26	668	310	358
27	782	409	373
28	811	414	397
29	832	414	418
30-34	4632	2296	2336
30	920	462	458
31	884	436	448
32	955	475	480
33	931	447	484
34	942	476	466
35-39	4332	2093	2239
35	881	436	445
36	926	440	486
37	861	428	433
38	881	420	461
39	783	369	414
40-44	3952	1971	1981
40	814	409	405
41	801	391	410
42	791	417	374
43	791	386	405
44	755	368	387
45-49	3879	1938	1941
45	820	429	391
46	790	385	405
47	748	377	371
48	791	378	413
49	730	369	361

Age	All Persons	Males	Females
50-54	3757	1856	1901
50	734	380	354
51	789	404	385
52	737	355	382
53	709	329	380
54	788	388	400
55-59	3476	1682	1794
55	746	357	389
56	678	340	338
57	731	370	361
58	687	310	377
59	634	305	329
60-64	2866	1384	1482
60	544	262	282
61	605	287	318
62	602	303	299
63	567	273	294
64	548	259	289
65-69	2502	1191	1311
65	540	263	277
66	527	239	288
67	502	248	254
68	492	227	265
69	441	214	227
70-74	2182	940	1242
70	461	180	281
71	449	197	252
72	456	212	244
73	376	165	211
74	440	186	254
75-79	1739	713	1026
75	398	166	232
76	357	159	198
77	339	141	198
78	351	126	225
79	294	121	173
80-84	1143	426	717
80	307	128	179
81	233	85	148
82	233	71	162
83	186	69	117
84	184	73	111
85-89	616	180	436
85	146	45	101
86	138	45	93
87	134	43	91
88	105	33	72
89	93	14	79
90 and over	280	61	219
Under 16	12884	6610	6274
Under 18	14645	7511	7134
16-44	23286	11590	11696
45-59/64*	12496	6860	5636
60/65** and over	9944	3511	6433

* 45 – 64 for males; 45 – 59 for females.
** 65 and over for males; 60 and over for females.

Table P2

Population at Census Day 2001: Resident population by single year of age and sex

Age	All Persons	Males	Females
All ages	26894	13323	13571
0-4	1928	988	940
0	359	173	186
1	382	210	172
2	394	214	180
3	388	173	215
4	405	218	187
5-9	1883	979	904
5	362	191	171
6	391	209	182
7	364	177	187
8	390	208	182
9	376	194	182
10-14	2150	1086	1064
10	438	202	236
11	440	227	213
12	395	208	187
13	427	223	204
14	450	226	224
15-19	1974	1006	968
15	409	227	182
16	455	236	219
17	412	204	208
18	387	176	211
19	311	163	148
20-24	1558	819	739
20	320	181	139
21	300	156	144
22	289	137	152
23	312	144	168
24	337	201	136
25-29	1882	957	925
25	325	147	178
26	322	160	162
27	352	185	167
28	400	195	205
29	483	270	213
30-34	2113	1083	1030
30	449	251	198
31	417	191	226
32	434	221	213
33	432	221	211
34	381	199	182
35-39	2086	1034	1052
35	426	203	223
36	446	239	207
37	404	211	193
38	370	178	192
39	440	203	237
40-44	1833	921	912
40	390	198	192
41	378	191	187
42	355	197	158
43	324	156	168
44	386	179	207
45-49	1631	827	804
45	387	201	186
46	319	161	158
47	325	164	161
48	296	159	137
49	304	142	162

Age	All Persons	Males	Females
50-54	1522	792	730
50	299	171	128
51	321	159	162
52	300	149	151
53	292	146	146
54	310	167	143
55-59	1485	710	775
55	281	136	145
56	290	142	148
57	319	159	160
58	325	158	167
59	270	115	155
60-64	1215	594	621
60	255	118	137
61	263	137	126
62	249	132	117
63	227	108	119
64	221	99	122
65-69	1031	480	551
65	196	82	114
66	227	109	118
67	218	102	116
68	203	97	106
69	187	90	97
70-74	966	425	541
70	212	95	117
71	202	96	106
72	186	74	112
73	183	79	104
74	183	81	102
75-79	779	332	447
75	159	65	94
76	159	72	87
77	166	74	92
78	152	58	94
79	143	63	80
80-84	540	200	340
80	137	56	81
81	138	55	83
82	103	34	69
83	88	26	62
84	74	29	45
85-89	219	67	152
85	57	15	42
86	47	16	31
87	41	11	30
88	45	19	26
89	29	6	23
90 and over	99	23	76
Under 16	6370	3280	3090
Under 18	7237	3720	3517
16-44	11037	5593	5444
45-59/64*	5232	2923	2309
60/65** and over	4255	1527	2728

* 45 – 64 for males; 45 – 59 for females.
** 65 and over for males; 60 and over for females.

Table P2

Population at Census Day 2001: Resident population by single year of age and sex

Age	All Persons	Males	Females
All ages	41392	20705	20687
0-4	2978	1571	1407
0	585	292	293
1	561	309	252
2	603	319	284
3	610	325	285
4	619	326	293
5-9	2998	1581	1417
5	586	299	287
6	641	357	284
7	587	313	274
8	586	317	269
9	598	295	303
10-14	3162	1663	1499
10	615	361	254
11	606	308	298
12	647	350	297
13	631	302	329
14	663	342	321
15-19	2992	1546	1446
15	642	326	316
16	643	316	327
17	595	328	267
18	600	324	276
19	512	252	260
20-24	2398	1210	1188
20	490	271	219
21	504	237	267
22	441	230	211
23	462	241	221
24	501	231	270
25-29	2882	1458	1424
25	522	282	240
26	506	254	252
27	572	279	293
28	600	303	297
29	682	340	342
30-34	3451	1800	1651
30	670	345	325
31	716	368	348
32	654	338	316
33	677	349	328
34	734	400	334
35-39	3431	1741	1690
35	680	339	341
36	695	362	333
37	704	365	339
38	669	352	317
39	683	323	360
40-44	2998	1480	1518
40	590	285	305
41	609	290	319
42	629	303	326
43	592	299	293
44	578	303	275
45-49	2609	1387	1222
45	607	322	285
46	531	290	241
47	508	266	242
48	511	289	222
49	452	220	232

Age	All Persons	Males	Females
50-54	2355	1134	1221
50	469	224	245
51	474	237	237
52	460	227	233
53	490	227	263
54	462	219	243
55-59	2186	1109	1077
55	435	223	212
56	469	252	217
57	421	222	199
58	455	227	228
59	406	185	221
60-64	1757	830	927
60	383	173	210
61	344	165	179
62	329	158	171
63	342	158	184
64	359	176	183
65-69	1570	724	846
65	335	160	175
66	294	135	159
67	325	147	178
68	300	136	164
69	316	146	170
70-74	1296	599	697
70	295	146	149
71	263	117	146
72	258	121	137
73	230	113	117
74	250	102	148
75-79	1056	434	622
75	251	116	135
76	223	97	126
77	209	77	132
78	187	72	115
79	186	72	114
80-84	722	271	451
80	175	65	110
81	170	63	107
82	152	56	96
83	127	47	80
84	98	40	58
85-89	392	132	260
85	108	33	75
86	99	35	64
87	65	26	39
88	74	30	44
89	46	8	38
90 and over	159	35	124
Under 16	9780	5141	4639
Under 18	11018	5785	5233
16-44	17510	8909	8601
45-59/64*	7980	4460	3520
60/65** and over	6122	2195	3927

*   45 – 64 for males; 45 – 59 for females.
**   65 and over for males; 60 and over for females.

Table P2

Population at Census Day 2001: Resident population by single year of age and sex

Age	All Persons	Males	Females	Age	All Persons	Males	Females
All ages	277391	129778	147613	50-54	14223	6845	7378
				50	2845	1390	1455
0-4	16616	8465	8151	51	2797	1324	1473
0	3293	1632	1661	52	2720	1326	1394
1	3090	1648	1442	53	2885	1409	1476
2	3292	1697	1595	54	2976	1396	1580
3	3337	1707	1630				
4	3604	1781	1823	55-59	13631	6526	7105
				55	2698	1327	1371
5-9	18722	9512	9210	56	2716	1305	1411
5	3388	1741	1647	57	2804	1326	1478
6	3564	1767	1797	58	2890	1363	1527
7	3764	1863	1901	59	2523	1205	1318
8	3939	2005	1934				
9	4067	2136	1931	60-64	12149	5693	6456
				60	2257	1096	1161
10-14	20588	10478	10110	61	2420	1141	1279
10	3973	2025	1948	62	2468	1132	1336
11	3931	1966	1965	63	2483	1160	1323
12	4166	2138	2028	64	2521	1164	1357
13	4276	2133	2143				
14	4242	2216	2026	65-69	11723	5153	6570
				65	2430	1054	1376
15-19	22650	11040	11610	66	2314	1028	1286
15	4335	2191	2144	67	2327	1046	1281
16	4296	2206	2090	68	2303	984	1319
17	4006	2048	1958	69	2349	1041	1308
18	4261	2155	2106				
19	5752	2440	3312	70-74	11035	4458	6577
				70	2384	948	1436
20-24	23261	11038	12223	71	2328	951	1377
20	5290	2409	2881	72	2104	865	1239
21	5039	2386	2653	73	2106	854	1252
22	4595	2188	2407	74	2113	840	1273
23	4191	2006	2185				
24	4146	2049	2097	75-79	8964	3325	5639
				75	2018	796	1222
25-29	20152	9580	10572	76	1929	760	1169
25	4229	2011	2218	77	1750	606	1144
26	4063	1945	2118	78	1648	600	1048
27	4043	1860	2183	79	1619	563	1056
28	4105	1976	2129				
29	3712	1788	1924	80-84	5847	1971	3876
				80	1578	561	1017
30-34	19652	9183	10469	81	1463	532	931
30	3990	1875	2115	82	1074	368	706
31	3893	1860	2033	83	884	255	629
32	3854	1762	2092	84	848	255	593
33	3851	1831	2020				
34	4064	1855	2209	85-89	3277	903	2374
				85	801	239	562
35-39	19825	9280	10545	86	800	236	564
35	3961	1873	2088	87	671	184	487
36	4053	1927	2126	88	564	134	430
37	4057	1908	2149	89	441	110	331
38	3871	1784	2087				
39	3883	1788	2095	90 and over	1523	295	1228
40-44	18366	8534	9832	Under 16	60261	30646	29615
40	3879	1821	2058				
41	3706	1740	1966	Under 18	68563	34900	33663
42	3638	1634	2004				
43	3649	1747	1902	16-44	119571	56464	63107
44	3494	1592	1902				
				45-59/64*	48734	26563	22171
45-49	15187	7499	7688				
45	3229	1565	1664	60/65** and over	48825	16105	32720
46	3047	1501	1546				
47	3064	1505	1559				
48	3032	1485	1547				
49	2815	1443	1372				

*   45 – 64 for males; 45 – 59 for females.
**   65 and over for males; 60 and over for females.

Table P2

Population at Census Day 2001: Resident population by single year of age and sex

Age	All Persons	Males	Females	Age	All Persons	Males	Females
All ages	37659	18239	19420	50-54	2194	1066	1128
				50	452	230	222
0-4	2436	1274	1162	51	451	235	216
0	484	259	225	52	381	172	209
1	469	242	227	53	450	215	235
2	475	244	231	54	460	214	246
3	501	264	237				
4	507	265	242	55-59	2082	1016	1066
				55	408	206	202
5-9	2684	1378	1306	56	429	217	212
5	522	262	260	57	440	190	250
6	534	285	249	58	423	227	196
7	541	279	262	59	382	176	206
8	530	253	277				
9	557	299	258	60-64	1677	828	849
				60	342	191	151
10-14	2790	1389	1401	61	342	164	178
10	522	240	282	62	320	149	171
11	587	300	287	63	344	168	176
12	552	272	280	64	329	156	173
13	557	285	272				
14	572	292	280	65-69	1517	695	822
				65	331	157	174
15-19	2612	1346	1266	66	299	139	160
15	609	310	299	67	319	137	182
16	549	302	247	68	295	140	155
17	493	254	239	69	273	122	151
18	509	273	236				
19	452	207	245	70-74	1291	565	726
				70	306	128	178
20-24	2198	1056	1142	71	258	118	140
20	492	268	224	72	245	110	135
21	417	211	206	73	237	99	138
22	397	180	217	74	245	110	135
23	466	209	257				
24	426	188	238	75-79	1057	409	648
				75	216	80	136
25-29	2398	1170	1228	76	213	97	116
25	388	171	217	77	229	95	134
26	451	225	226	78	206	72	134
27	472	233	239	79	193	65	128
28	556	290	266				
29	531	251	280	80-84	647	237	410
				80	174	62	112
30-34	3026	1435	1591	81	164	63	101
30	567	252	315	82	112	39	73
31	606	288	318	83	101	31	70
32	625	314	311	84	96	42	54
33	607	293	314				
34	621	288	333	85-89	314	85	229
				85	85	22	63
35-39	3273	1618	1655	86	75	27	48
35	671	343	328	87	61	16	45
36	687	331	356	88	53	10	43
37	677	342	335	89	40	10	30
38	641	309	332				
39	597	293	304	90 and over	171	24	147
40-44	2854	1395	1459	Under 16	8519	4351	4168
40	592	289	303				
41	608	287	321	Under 18	9561	4907	4654
42	595	300	295				
43	530	264	266	16-44	15752	7710	8042
44	529	255	274				
				45-59/64*	7542	4163	3379
45-49	2438	1253	1185				
45	495	216	279	60/65** and over	5846	2015	3831
46	473	240	233				
47	476	244	232				
48	505	264	241				
49	489	289	200				

*   45 – 64 for males; 45 – 59 for females.
** 65 and over for males; 60 and over for females.

Table P2

Population at Census Day 2001: Resident population by single year of age and sex

Age	All Persons	Males	Females	Age	All Persons	Males	Females
All ages	66488	31669	34819	50-54	3751	1804	1947
				50	734	366	368
0-4	4370	2227	2143	51	746	379	367
0	841	424	417	52	718	355	363
1	815	397	418	53	726	334	392
2	881	467	414	54	827	370	457
3	888	454	434				
4	945	485	460	55-59	3593	1695	1898
				55	705	346	359
5-9	4676	2398	2278	56	711	322	389
5	886	453	433	57	729	335	394
6	931	469	462	58	735	357	378
7	894	444	450	59	713	335	378
8	937	511	426				
9	1028	521	507	60-64	3136	1465	1671
				60	621	277	344
10-14	4581	2289	2292	61	597	290	307
10	951	446	505	62	645	307	338
11	958	495	463	63	601	288	313
12	915	460	455	64	672	303	369
13	861	445	416				
14	896	443	453	65-69	3036	1353	1683
				65	626	267	359
15-19	3756	1913	1843	66	569	269	300
15	834	426	408	67	578	270	308
16	818	391	427	68	641	264	377
17	741	358	383	69	622	283	339
18	713	387	326				
19	650	351	299	70-74	3027	1316	1711
				70	656	297	359
20-24	3072	1543	1529	71	630	268	362
20	617	335	282	72	610	274	336
21	655	354	301	73	549	238	311
22	613	292	321	74	582	239	343
23	588	288	300				
24	599	274	325	75-79	2396	971	1425
				75	527	210	317
25-29	3948	1900	2048	76	482	204	278
25	651	313	338	77	521	223	298
26	685	324	361	78	443	180	263
27	785	392	393	79	423	154	269
28	896	408	488				
29	931	463	468	80-84	1470	552	918
				80	399	156	243
30-34	5423	2558	2865	81	375	150	225
30	974	452	522	82	265	109	156
31	1011	481	530	83	225	69	156
32	1079	494	585	84	206	68	138
33	1160	554	606				
34	1199	577	622	85-89	685	211	474
				85	195	59	136
35-39	5959	2833	3126	86	166	49	117
35	1164	540	624	87	116	39	77
36	1222	577	645	88	131	41	90
37	1231	585	646	89	77	23	54
38	1196	597	599				
39	1146	534	612	90 and over	321	69	252
40-44	5166	2500	2666	Under 16	14461	7340	7121
40	1145	561	584				
41	1082	528	554	Under 18	16020	8089	7931
42	1041	506	535				
43	961	480	481	16-44	26490	12821	13669
44	937	425	512				
				45-59/64*	12931	7036	5895
45-49	4122	2072	2050				
45	927	450	477	60/65** and over	12606	4472	8134
46	822	410	412				
47	813	426	387				
48	811	405	406				
49	749	381	368				

*   45 – 64 for males; 45 – 59 for females.
**   65 and over for males; 60 and over for females.

Table P2

Population at Census Day 2001: Resident population by single year of age and sex

Age	All Persons	Males	Females	Age	All Persons	Males	Females
All ages	56315	26877	29438	50-54	3413	1666	1747
				50	648	330	318
0-4	3777	1920	1857	51	680	326	354
0	678	347	331	52	692	336	356
1	723	368	355	53	674	329	345
2	779	397	382	54	719	345	374
3	791	396	395				
4	806	412	394	55-59	3077	1543	1534
				55	608	327	281
5-9	3786	1910	1876	56	622	292	330
5	740	371	369	57	622	328	294
6	754	377	377	58	646	303	343
7	762	382	380	59	579	293	286
8	777	401	376				
9	753	379	374	60-64	2826	1293	1533
				60	593	272	321
10-14	4167	2155	2012	61	568	267	301
10	818	415	403	62	549	250	299
11	815	413	402	63	547	256	291
12	853	447	406	64	569	248	321
13	796	411	385				
14	885	469	416	65-69	2369	1116	1253
				65	492	238	254
15-19	4150	2039	2111	66	458	219	239
15	853	454	399	67	464	223	241
16	836	437	399	68	487	236	251
17	773	390	383	69	468	200	268
18	772	373	399				
19	916	385	531	70-74	1963	847	1116
				70	450	190	260
20-24	3986	1770	2216	71	425	183	242
20	974	394	580	72	386	183	203
21	907	408	499	73	331	126	205
22	773	345	428	74	371	165	206
23	682	304	378				
24	650	319	331	75-79	1688	709	979
				75	400	169	231
25-29	3447	1593	1854	76	345	158	187
25	617	292	325	77	321	134	187
26	597	263	334	78	307	125	182
27	699	331	368	79	315	123	192
28	767	343	424				
29	767	364	403	80-84	1113	403	710
				80	276	98	178
30-34	4046	1951	2095	81	249	95	154
30	818	396	422	82	213	74	139
31	732	362	370	83	209	82	127
32	784	373	411	84	166	54	112
33	839	400	439				
34	873	420	453	85-89	603	156	447
				85	131	35	96
35-39	4213	2016	2197	86	130	39	91
35	856	427	429	87	149	39	110
36	874	396	478	88	111	26	85
37	868	423	445	89	82	17	65
38	791	381	410				
39	824	389	435	90 and over	239	58	181
40-44	3998	1997	2001	Under 16	12583	6439	6144
40	807	406	401				
41	812	386	426	Under 18	14192	7266	6926
42	810	409	401				
43	769	370	399	16-44	22987	10912	12075
44	800	426	374				
				45-59/64*	11237	6237	5000
45-49	3454	1735	1719				
45	741	335	406	60/65** and over	9508	3289	6219
46	667	354	313				
47	724	377	347				
48	692	367	325				
49	630	302	328				

*   45 – 64 for males; 45 – 59 for females.
**   65 and over for males; 60 and over for females.

Table P2

Population at Census Day 2001: Resident population by single year of age and sex

Age	All Persons	Males	Females	Age	All Persons	Males	Females
All ages	32581	16188	16393	50-54	1849	917	932
				50	387	193	194
0-4	2363	1227	1136	51	359	178	181
0	414	232	182	52	357	168	189
1	485	237	248	53	374	183	191
2	479	238	241	54	372	195	177
3	468	254	214				
4	517	266	251	55-59	1665	824	841
				55	349	160	189
5-9	2572	1305	1267	56	352	176	176
5	494	273	221	57	351	181	170
6	524	266	258	58	321	166	155
7	497	248	249	59	292	141	151
8	521	255	266				
9	536	263	273	60-64	1324	643	681
				60	287	158	129
10-14	2913	1490	1423	61	291	134	157
10	576	294	282	62	257	120	137
11	582	299	283	63	255	121	134
12	584	299	285	64	234	110	124
13	582	296	286				
14	589	302	287	65-69	1063	509	554
				65	236	117	119
15-19	2754	1410	1344	66	215	114	101
15	607	321	286	67	216	103	113
16	639	332	307	68	202	94	108
17	589	286	303	69	194	81	113
18	543	271	272				
19	376	200	176	70-74	973	466	507
				70	185	99	86
20-24	2208	1168	1040	71	220	109	111
20	466	244	222	72	208	91	117
21	446	229	217	73	169	81	88
22	423	226	197	74	191	86	105
23	441	232	209				
24	432	237	195	75-79	804	347	457
				75	165	77	88
25-29	2335	1165	1170	76	169	78	91
25	482	234	248	77	182	84	98
26	427	208	219	78	130	45	85
27	459	239	220	79	158	63	95
28	482	240	242				
29	485	244	241	80-84	528	191	337
				80	134	54	80
30-34	2317	1140	1177	81	134	46	88
30	506	253	253	82	108	45	63
31	458	237	221	83	75	22	53
32	429	206	223	84	77	24	53
33	479	234	245				
34	445	210	235	85-89	267	81	186
				85	67	21	46
35-39	2375	1188	1187	86	68	19	49
35	478	222	256	87	48	18	30
36	495	252	243	88	59	17	42
37	502	255	247	89	25	6	19
38	464	262	202				
39	436	197	239	90 and over	110	35	75
40-44	2227	1110	1117	Under 16	8455	4343	4112
40	453	219	234				
41	474	226	248	Under 18	9683	4961	4722
42	419	245	174				
43	441	195	246	16-44	13609	6860	6749
44	440	225	215				
45-49	1934	972	962	45-59/64*	6091	3356	2735
45	404	198	206				
46	388	201	187	60/65** and over	4426	1629	2797
47	374	186	188				
48	395	216	179				
49	373	171	202				

*   45 – 64 for males; 45 – 59 for females.
** 65 and over for males; 60 and over for females.

Table P2

Population at Census Day 2001: Resident population by single year of age and sex

Age	All Persons	Males	Females	Age	All Persons	Males	Females
All ages	80671	39753	40918	50-54	4685	2309	2376
				50	897	475	422
0-4	5731	2969	2762	51	954	470	484
0	1053	562	491	52	943	486	457
1	1124	601	523	53	943	437	506
2	1136	582	554	54	948	441	507
3	1196	594	602				
4	1222	630	592	55-59	4319	2090	2229
				55	892	416	476
5-9	6273	3289	2984	56	895	427	468
5	1198	641	557	57	872	441	431
6	1199	633	566	58	920	438	482
7	1282	655	627	59	740	368	372
8	1287	658	629				
9	1307	702	605	60-64	3583	1701	1882
				60	719	384	335
10-14	6608	3465	3143	61	696	333	363
10	1350	722	628	62	751	338	413
11	1295	688	607	63	713	325	388
12	1307	700	607	64	704	321	383
13	1371	696	675				
14	1285	659	626	65-69	3125	1449	1676
				65	684	339	345
15-19	5970	3078	2892	66	635	293	342
15	1312	718	594	67	619	262	357
16	1334	636	698	68	603	289	314
17	1283	648	635	69	584	266	318
18	1156	594	562				
19	885	482	403	70-74	2627	1171	1456
				70	576	253	323
20-24	4672	2318	2354	71	563	267	296
20	917	474	443	72	520	229	291
21	966	499	467	73	500	213	287
22	950	453	497	74	468	209	259
23	920	446	474				
24	919	446	473	75-79	2091	820	1271
				75	467	191	276
25-29	5319	2696	2623	76	443	169	274
25	984	473	511	77	432	192	240
26	1014	509	505	78	396	144	252
27	1027	511	516	79	353	124	229
28	1106	603	503				
29	1188	600	588	80-84	1356	507	849
				80	366	144	222
30-34	6386	3169	3217	81	326	127	199
30	1178	573	605	82	281	108	173
31	1247	657	590	83	190	58	132
32	1312	663	649	84	193	70	123
33	1307	641	666				
34	1342	635	707	85-89	702	220	482
				85	205	68	137
35-39	6491	3229	3262	86	151	45	106
35	1331	664	667	87	139	44	95
36	1366	659	707	88	116	37	79
37	1306	654	652	89	91	26	65
38	1263	627	636				
39	1225	625	600	90 and over	293	61	232
40-44	5669	2819	2850	Under 16	19924	10441	9483
40	1186	605	581				
41	1249	634	615	Under 18	22541	11725	10816
42	1079	534	545				
43	1112	554	558	16-44	33195	16591	16604
44	1043	492	551				
				45-59/64*	15476	8493	6983
45-49	4771	2393	2378				
45	979	469	510	60/65** and over	12076	4228	7848
46	955	512	443				
47	958	476	482				
48	991	505	486				
49	888	431	457				

*   45 – 64 for males; 45 – 59 for females.
**   65 and over for males; 60 and over for females.

Table P2

Population at Census Day 2001: Resident population by single year of age and sex

Age	All Persons	Males	Females	Age	All Persons	Males	Females
All ages	105066	51137	53929	50-54	5678	2835	2843
				50	1191	576	615
0-4	8060	4170	3890	51	1161	595	566
0	1467	747	720	52	1120	577	543
1	1545	825	720	53	1107	529	578
2	1631	828	803	54	1099	558	541
3	1670	882	788				
4	1747	888	859	55-59	4723	2299	2424
				55	982	498	484
5-9	8568	4300	4268	56	934	436	498
5	1733	881	852	57	1043	498	545
6	1652	836	816	58	963	468	495
7	1657	836	821	59	801	399	402
8	1781	869	912				
9	1745	878	867	60-64	3989	1960	2029
				60	832	412	420
10-14	9638	4903	4735	61	775	372	403
10	1864	928	936	62	792	382	410
11	1819	928	891	63	811	427	384
12	1915	979	936	64	779	367	412
13	2064	1049	1015				
14	1976	1019	957	65-69	3307	1526	1781
				65	742	342	400
15-19	9380	4908	4472	66	681	329	352
15	1939	1040	899	67	628	286	342
16	1976	1030	946	68	645	292	353
17	2005	1029	976	69	611	277	334
18	1821	948	873				
19	1639	861	778	70-74	2783	1238	1545
				70	629	287	342
20-24	7663	3821	3842	71	539	239	300
20	1608	805	803	72	588	250	338
21	1615	819	796	73	519	234	285
22	1494	726	768	74	508	228	280
23	1458	713	745				
24	1488	758	730	75-79	2043	766	1277
				75	488	193	295
25-29	7544	3596	3948	76	436	165	271
25	1474	715	759	77	395	158	237
26	1486	709	777	78	368	128	240
27	1504	723	781	79	356	122	234
28	1534	718	816				
29	1546	731	815	80-84	1234	434	800
				80	336	117	219
30-34	8190	3927	4263	81	294	102	192
30	1603	757	846	82	240	93	147
31	1618	784	834	83	196	72	124
32	1668	825	843	84	168	50	118
33	1682	789	893				
34	1619	772	847	85-89	651	174	477
				85	174	62	112
35-39	8212	3921	4291	86	142	44	98
35	1700	775	925	87	132	25	107
36	1677	825	852	88	104	18	86
37	1598	777	821	89	99	25	74
38	1638	766	872				
39	1599	778	821	90 and over	268	60	208
40-44	7082	3389	3693	Under 16	28205	14413	13792
40	1579	756	823				
41	1474	723	751	Under 18	32186	16472	15714
42	1383	658	725				
43	1364	647	717	16-44	46132	22522	23610
44	1282	605	677				
45-49	6053	2910	3143	45-59/64*	18414	10004	8410
45	1276	619	657				
46	1274	643	631	60/65** and over	12315	4198	8117
47	1219	557	662				
48	1157	558	599				
49	1127	533	594				

*   45 – 64 for males; 45 – 59 for females.
**   65 and over for males; 60 and over for females.

Table P2

Population at Census Day 2001: Resident population by single year of age and sex

Age	All Persons	Males	Females	Age	All Persons	Males	Females
All ages	63828	31622	32206	50-54	3852	1946	1906
				50	790	393	397
0-4	4424	2261	2163	51	803	408	395
0	830	401	429	52	751	382	369
1	842	454	388	53	805	418	387
2	884	465	419	54	703	345	358
3	946	498	448				
4	922	443	479	55-59	3342	1696	1646
				55	707	354	353
5-9	5039	2577	2462	56	692	356	336
5	979	515	464	57	681	327	354
6	959	505	454	58	685	358	327
7	1006	482	524	59	577	301	276
8	1016	500	516				
9	1079	575	504	60-64	2764	1339	1425
				60	587	273	314
10-14	5310	2701	2609	61	539	272	267
10	1060	546	514	62	558	286	272
11	1085	559	526	63	524	246	278
12	1033	512	521	64	556	262	294
13	1073	560	513				
14	1059	524	535	65-69	2376	1111	1265
				65	508	242	266
15-19	5157	2696	2461	66	503	251	252
15	1092	573	519	67	478	229	249
16	1114	570	544	68	479	206	273
17	1041	543	498	69	408	183	225
18	1045	539	506				
19	865	471	394	70-74	1998	881	1117
				70	425	204	221
20-24	3882	2096	1786	71	418	192	226
20	807	467	340	72	394	175	219
21	775	433	342	73	393	160	233
22	782	399	383	74	368	150	218
23	783	409	374				
24	735	388	347	75-79	1675	662	1013
				75	366	142	224
25-29	3963	2024	1939	76	364	144	220
25	788	418	370	77	327	132	195
26	732	370	362	78	308	124	184
27	756	382	374	79	310	120	190
28	844	418	426				
29	843	436	407	80-84	1107	442	665
				80	285	129	156
30-34	4675	2315	2360	81	274	114	160
30	930	458	472	82	187	75	112
31	867	413	454	83	194	66	128
32	984	484	500	84	167	58	109
33	945	460	485				
34	949	500	449	85-89	613	184	429
				85	143	52	91
35-39	4988	2465	2523	86	141	34	107
35	1038	511	527	87	119	36	83
36	1024	499	525	88	107	28	79
37	979	482	497	89	103	34	69
38	946	482	464				
39	1001	491	510	90 and over	319	73	246
40-44	4387	2191	2196	Under 16	15865	8112	7753
40	858	419	439				
41	922	476	446	Under 18	18020	9225	8795
42	885	434	451				
43	903	443	460	16-44	25960	13214	12746
44	819	419	400				
				45-59/64*	12490	6943	5547
45-49	3957	1962	1995				
45	859	420	439	60/65** and over	9513	3353	6160
46	782	389	393				
47	821	407	414				
48	744	374	370				
49	751	372	379				

*   45 – 64 for males; 45 – 59 for females.
** 65 and over for males; 60 and over for females.

Table P2

Population at Census Day 2001: Resident population by single year of age and sex

Age	All Persons	Males	Females	Age	All Persons	Males	Females
All ages	47735	23624	24111	50-54	2696	1320	1376
				50	544	265	279
0-4	3586	1823	1763	51	539	261	278
0	669	342	327	52	552	284	268
1	725	366	359	53	549	262	287
2	743	349	394	54	512	248	264
3	706	386	320				
4	743	380	363	55-59	2340	1166	1174
				55	500	258	242
5-9	3753	1910	1843	56	475	218	257
5	701	348	353	57	476	241	235
6	721	392	329	58	449	232	217
7	757	384	373	59	440	217	223
8	755	388	367				
9	819	398	421	60-64	2005	978	1027
				60	417	187	230
10-14	4138	2092	2046	61	399	212	187
10	826	417	409	62	425	195	230
11	818	419	399	63	376	193	183
12	812	412	400	64	388	191	197
13	781	365	416				
14	901	479	422	65-69	1803	850	953
				65	389	199	190
15-19	3881	1982	1899	66	340	159	181
15	838	437	401	67	338	164	174
16	827	426	401	68	385	163	222
17	881	443	438	69	351	165	186
18	784	381	403				
19	551	295	256	70-74	1571	668	903
				70	364	144	220
20-24	3000	1542	1458	71	305	135	170
20	544	304	240	72	294	137	157
21	595	319	276	73	338	133	205
22	636	334	302	74	270	119	151
23	574	294	280				
24	651	291	360	75-79	1249	521	728
				75	277	126	151
25-29	3454	1736	1718	76	295	121	174
25	676	347	329	77	231	99	132
26	634	337	297	78	243	93	150
27	722	357	365	79	203	82	121
28	756	370	386				
29	666	325	341	80-84	778	284	494
				80	198	65	133
30-34	3502	1795	1707	81	165	67	98
30	761	425	336	82	143	61	82
31	667	348	319	83	131	45	86
32	680	306	374	84	141	46	95
33	716	370	346				
34	678	346	332	85-89	385	118	267
				85	103	26	77
35-39	3374	1688	1686	86	91	33	58
35	695	347	348	87	81	22	59
36	662	334	328	88	62	22	40
37	680	331	349	89	48	15	33
38	655	327	328				
39	682	349	333	90 and over	173	43	130
40-44	3211	1627	1584	Under 16	12315	6262	6053
40	698	360	338				
41	674	346	328	Under 18	14023	7131	6892
42	604	303	301				
43	621	311	310	16-44	19584	9933	9651
44	614	307	307				
				45-59/64*	8850	4945	3905
45-49	2836	1481	1355				
45	603	312	291	60/65** and over	6986	2484	4502
46	594	315	279				
47	581	305	276				
48	520	257	263				
49	538	292	246				

*   45 – 64 for males; 45 – 59 for females.
** 65 and over for males; 60 and over for females.

Table P2

Population at Census Day 2001: Resident population by single year of age and sex

Age	All Persons	Males	Females
All ages	57527	28818	28709
0-4	3929	1979	1950
0	763	393	370
1	732	353	379
2	817	421	396
3	810	389	421
4	807	423	384
5-9	4083	2189	1894
5	814	439	375
6	785	418	367
7	859	465	394
8	816	440	376
9	809	427	382
10-14	4786	2443	2343
10	932	473	459
11	930	460	470
12	975	491	484
13	932	515	417
14	1017	504	513
15-19	4751	2389	2362
15	1066	527	539
16	1036	515	521
17	1068	538	530
18	951	466	485
19	630	343	287
20-24	3270	1732	1538
20	649	351	298
21	597	347	250
22	692	361	331
23	671	344	327
24	661	329	332
25-29	3753	1922	1831
25	679	342	337
26	690	352	338
27	750	382	368
28	798	405	393
29	836	441	395
30-34	3988	2036	1952
30	813	406	407
31	822	407	415
32	792	408	384
33	791	412	379
34	770	403	367
35-39	4152	2113	2039
35	813	391	422
36	870	470	400
37	850	422	428
38	825	423	402
39	794	407	387
40-44	4026	2013	2013
40	842	419	423
41	812	407	405
42	772	371	401
43	827	415	412
44	773	401	372
45-49	3832	1993	1839
45	835	435	400
46	755	396	359
47	771	404	367
48	731	373	358
49	740	385	355

Age	All Persons	Males	Females
50-54	3599	1799	1800
50	711	363	348
51	687	348	339
52	770	365	405
53	693	348	345
54	738	375	363
55-59	2950	1511	1439
55	604	324	280
56	606	302	304
57	611	336	275
58	590	275	315
59	539	274	265
60-64	2449	1259	1190
60	457	232	225
61	500	267	233
62	501	268	233
63	479	237	242
64	512	255	257
65-69	2223	1070	1153
65	443	204	239
66	454	222	232
67	475	226	249
68	410	196	214
69	441	222	219
70-74	1971	912	1059
70	384	184	200
71	394	187	207
72	406	191	215
73	363	151	212
74	424	199	225
75-79	1719	713	1006
75	375	169	206
76	343	135	208
77	368	151	217
78	348	138	210
79	285	120	165
80-84	1150	455	695
80	273	120	153
81	262	101	161
82	242	101	141
83	190	73	117
84	183	60	123
85-89	638	217	421
85	168	49	119
86	137	45	92
87	127	45	82
88	120	48	72
89	86	30	56
90 and over	258	73	185
Under 16	13864	7138	6726
Under 18	15968	8191	7777
16-44	22874	11678	11196
45-59/64*	11640	6562	5078
60/65** and over	9149	3440	5709

*   45 – 64 for males; 45 – 59 for females.
**   65 and over for males; 60 and over for females.

Table P2

Population at Census Day 2001: Resident population by single year of age and sex

Age	All Persons	Males	Females	Age	All Persons	Males	Females
All ages	30832	15125	15707	50-54	2039	991	1048
				50	399	187	212
0-4	1908	990	918	51	396	181	215
0	343	163	180	52	383	195	188
1	393	209	184	53	416	205	211
2	377	199	178	54	445	223	222
3	372	205	167				
4	423	214	209	55-59	1839	936	903
				55	366	195	171
5-9	2104	1049	1055	56	339	177	162
5	399	204	195	57	397	191	206
6	394	213	181	58	405	211	194
7	411	205	206	59	332	162	170
8	438	209	229				
9	462	218	244	60-64	1541	739	802
				60	306	148	158
10-14	2254	1197	1057	61	318	149	169
10	461	257	204	62	309	160	149
11	428	227	201	63	294	150	144
12	462	251	211	64	314	132	182
13	468	239	229				
14	435	223	212	65-69	1385	673	712
				65	277	129	148
15-19	2085	1034	1051	66	300	133	167
15	457	217	240	67	268	140	128
16	438	214	224	68	294	139	155
17	465	236	229	69	246	132	114
18	396	192	204				
19	329	175	154	70-74	1151	498	653
				70	279	123	156
20-24	1532	752	780	71	234	103	131
20	315	153	162	72	219	93	126
21	312	155	157	73	209	86	123
22	304	150	154	74	210	93	117
23	293	133	160				
24	308	161	147	75-79	918	380	538
				75	200	90	110
25-29	1843	889	954	76	176	79	97
25	300	154	146	77	187	75	112
26	369	173	196	78	171	68	103
27	363	192	171	79	184	68	116
28	407	190	217				
29	404	180	224	80-84	643	245	398
				80	153	65	88
30-34	2325	1154	1171	81	156	60	96
30	430	212	218	82	143	46	97
31	476	239	237	83	100	40	60
32	459	229	230	84	91	34	57
33	462	232	230				
34	498	242	256	85-89	313	78	235
				85	75	32	43
35-39	2522	1235	1287	86	85	17	68
35	482	233	249	87	57	11	46
36	509	253	256	88	51	11	40
37	524	248	276	89	45	7	38
38	511	257	254				
39	496	244	252	90 and over	149	29	120
40-44	2349	1227	1122	Under 16	6723	3453	3270
40	484	285	199				
41	485	244	241	Under 18	7626	3903	3723
42	483	244	239				
43	475	246	229	16-44	12199	6074	6125
44	422	208	214				
				45-59/64*	6549	3695	2854
45-49	1932	1029	903				
45	416	210	206	60/65** and over	5361	1903	3458
46	377	211	166				
47	369	217	152				
48	384	181	203				
49	386	210	176				

* 45 – 64 for males; 45 – 59 for females.
** 65 and over for males; 60 and over for females.

Table P2

Population at Census Day 2001: Resident population by single year of age and sex

Age	All Persons	Males	Females
All ages	32422	16497	15925
0-4	2462	1246	1216
0	455	211	244
1	470	249	221
2	525	254	271
3	485	229	256
4	527	303	224
5-9	2581	1334	1247
5	510	269	241
6	537	268	269
7	481	254	227
8	494	256	238
9	559	287	272
10-14	2685	1412	1273
10	551	298	253
11	529	294	235
12	531	267	264
13	536	270	266
14	538	283	255
15-19	2641	1370	1271
15	556	292	264
16	508	247	261
17	554	295	259
18	548	283	265
19	475	253	222
20-24	2253	1218	1035
20	421	225	196
21	426	235	191
22	420	233	187
23	459	235	224
24	527	290	237
25-29	2666	1372	1294
25	523	263	260
26	503	262	241
27	532	273	259
28	549	287	262
29	559	287	272
30-34	2676	1379	1297
30	545	280	265
31	523	266	257
32	549	266	283
33	527	287	240
34	532	280	252
35-39	2554	1334	1220
35	578	315	263
36	559	279	280
37	472	246	226
38	487	264	223
39	458	230	228
40-44	2121	1102	1019
40	479	250	229
41	430	219	211
42	424	199	225
43	392	212	180
44	396	222	174
45-49	2002	1054	948
45	396	220	176
46	471	265	206
47	385	194	191
48	384	205	179
49	366	170	196

Age	All Persons	Males	Females
50-54	1789	911	878
50	378	190	188
51	370	184	186
52	360	192	168
53	323	170	153
54	358	175	183
55-59	1577	762	815
55	341	158	183
56	348	184	164
57	322	161	161
58	290	122	168
59	276	137	139
60-64	1254	648	606
60	268	142	126
61	221	121	100
62	288	144	144
63	238	122	116
64	239	119	120
65-69	942	456	486
65	196	97	99
66	185	88	97
67	178	79	99
68	181	91	90
69	202	101	101
70-74	842	376	466
70	169	89	80
71	178	83	95
72	180	73	107
73	167	70	97
74	148	61	87
75-79	672	266	406
75	154	64	90
76	120	51	69
77	152	62	90
78	133	46	87
79	113	43	70
80-84	408	168	240
80	110	53	57
81	94	40	54
82	96	38	58
83	54	14	40
84	54	23	31
85-89	214	67	147
85	55	16	39
86	50	18	32
87	50	15	35
88	36	11	25
89	23	7	16
90 and over	83	22	61
Under 16	8284	4284	4000
Under 18	9346	4826	4520
16-44	14355	7483	6872
45-59/64*	6016	3375	2641
60/65** and over	3767	1355	2412

*   45 – 64 for males; 45 – 59 for females.
**   65 and over for males; 60 and over for females.

Table P2

Population at Census Day 2001: Resident population by single year of age and sex

Age	All Persons	Males	Females
All ages	108694	52979	55715
0-4	7808	4112	3696
0	1453	786	667
1	1497	785	712
2	1581	791	790
3	1587	840	747
4	1690	910	780
5-9	8561	4453	4108
5	1726	911	815
6	1684	881	803
7	1621	837	784
8	1734	884	850
9	1796	940	856
10-14	8611	4415	4196
10	1761	893	868
11	1742	881	861
12	1696	865	831
13	1708	903	805
14	1704	873	831
15-19	8084	4107	3977
15	1674	846	828
16	1760	908	852
17	1679	831	848
18	1582	804	778
19	1389	718	671
20-24	6516	3281	3235
20	1401	746	655
21	1298	722	576
22	1288	618	670
23	1209	563	646
24	1320	632	688
25-29	7066	3480	3586
25	1291	655	636
26	1341	677	664
27	1405	671	734
28	1474	701	773
29	1555	776	779
30-34	8714	4185	4529
30	1688	812	876
31	1652	780	872
32	1749	825	924
33	1757	862	895
34	1868	906	962
35-39	8975	4302	4673
35	1805	906	899
36	1873	893	980
37	1762	832	930
38	1786	845	941
39	1749	826	923
40-44	7940	3837	4103
40	1760	836	924
41	1619	780	839
42	1527	731	796
43	1569	774	795
44	1465	716	749
45-49	6744	3381	3363
45	1481	766	715
46	1332	679	653
47	1362	700	662
48	1303	619	684
49	1266	617	649

Age	All Persons	Males	Females
50-54	6481	3173	3308
50	1214	618	596
51	1278	640	638
52	1370	647	723
53	1315	624	691
54	1304	644	660
55-59	5708	2793	2915
55	1114	565	549
56	1203	593	610
57	1200	563	637
58	1208	580	628
59	983	492	491
60-64	4570	2166	2404
60	956	464	492
61	959	445	514
62	964	452	512
63	843	412	431
64	848	393	455
65-69	3990	1866	2124
65	850	415	435
66	807	387	420
67	786	364	422
68	771	352	419
69	776	348	428
70-74	3362	1466	1896
70	717	347	370
71	686	285	401
72	682	280	402
73	628	256	372
74	649	298	351
75-79	2578	1039	1539
75	611	252	359
76	531	223	308
77	499	195	304
78	468	178	290
79	469	191	278
80-84	1676	598	1078
80	469	177	292
81	408	163	245
82	318	102	216
83	245	78	167
84	236	78	158
85-89	882	250	632
85	235	58	177
86	170	53	117
87	193	60	133
88	171	51	120
89	113	28	85
90 and over	428	75	353
Under 16	26654	13826	12828
Under 18	30093	15565	14528
16-44	45621	22346	23275
45-59/64*	21099	11513	9586
60/65** and over	15320	5294	10026

* 45 – 64 for males; 45 – 59 for females.
** 65 and over for males; 60 and over for females.

Table P2

Population at Census Day 2001: Resident population by single year of age and sex

Age	All Persons	Males	Females	Age	All Persons	Males	Females
All ages	39780	20041	19739	50-54	2146	1075	1071
				50	467	243	224
0-4	3038	1569	1469	51	419	204	215
0	565	302	263	52	400	188	212
1	621	311	310	53	423	233	190
2	598	299	299	54	437	207	230
3	653	354	299				
4	601	303	298	55-59	1876	918	958
				55	397	205	192
5-9	3174	1602	1572	56	416	194	222
5	676	348	328	57	367	189	178
6	614	310	304	58	357	177	180
7	619	313	306	59	339	153	186
8	614	323	291				
9	651	308	343	60-64	1508	734	774
				60	311	169	142
10-14	3447	1777	1670	61	338	160	178
10	642	333	309	62	309	136	173
11	690	333	357	63	270	119	151
12	726	394	332	64	280	150	130
13	689	362	327				
14	700	355	345	65-69	1382	669	713
				65	284	139	145
15-19	3169	1633	1536	66	273	129	144
15	705	354	351	67	295	154	141
16	688	369	319	68	269	122	147
17	670	321	349	69	261	125	136
18	660	340	320				
19	446	249	197	70-74	1182	541	641
				70	263	119	144
20-24	2735	1467	1268	71	257	127	130
20	470	230	240	72	211	101	110
21	509	255	254	73	229	103	126
22	630	373	257	74	222	91	131
23	544	296	248				
24	582	313	269	75-79	905	394	511
				75	209	101	108
25-29	3124	1650	1474	76	183	90	93
25	637	356	281	77	177	67	110
26	575	289	286	78	171	59	112
27	709	410	299	79	165	77	88
28	576	280	296				
29	627	315	312	80-84	651	267	384
				80	149	69	80
30-34	3139	1628	1511	81	171	68	103
30	667	362	305	82	122	46	76
31	656	332	324	83	111	50	61
32	618	313	305	84	98	34	64
33	621	311	310				
34	577	310	267	85-89	321	113	208
				85	75	28	47
35-39	2934	1493	1441	86	76	23	53
35	628	317	311	87	67	20	47
36	585	303	282	88	49	20	29
37	606	297	309	89	54	22	32
38	560	301	259				
39	555	275	280	90 and over	115	40	75
40-44	2619	1275	1344	Under 16	10364	5302	5062
40	561	259	302				
41	517	257	260	Under 18	11722	5992	5730
42	514	252	262				
43	523	253	270	16-44	17015	8792	8223
44	504	254	250				
				45-59/64*	7071	3923	3148
45-49	2315	1196	1119				
45	482	244	238	60/65** and over	5330	2024	3306
46	459	226	233				
47	492	274	218				
48	435	232	203	* 45 – 64 for males; 45 – 59 for females.			
49	447	220	227	** 65 and over for males; 60 and over for females.			

CENSUS

Table P2

Population at Census Day 2001: Resident population by single year of age and sex

Age	All Persons	Males	Females
All ages	15933	7831	8102
0-4	1109	580	529
0	210	109	101
1	209	108	101
2	235	131	104
3	213	110	103
4	242	122	120
5-9	1077	541	536
5	193	106	87
6	205	101	104
7	218	95	123
8	226	121	105
9	235	118	117
10-14	1295	667	628
10	257	130	127
11	254	134	120
12	245	117	128
13	261	141	120
14	278	145	133
15-19	1266	657	609
15	295	141	154
16	278	155	123
17	261	127	134
18	236	132	104
19	196	102	94
20-24	851	420	431
20	192	93	99
21	167	85	82
22	186	92	94
23	149	81	68
24	157	69	88
25-29	1003	481	522
25	189	93	96
26	198	90	108
27	189	88	101
28	211	112	99
29	216	98	118
30-34	1084	561	523
30	209	110	99
31	227	122	105
32	224	123	101
33	216	100	116
34	208	106	102
35-39	1085	516	569
35	199	88	111
36	230	105	125
37	233	115	118
38	220	110	110
39	203	98	105
40-44	1089	526	563
40	232	127	105
41	213	115	98
42	221	103	118
43	216	99	117
44	207	82	125
45-49	1059	568	491
45	191	101	90
46	216	113	103
47	199	112	87
48	226	114	112
49	227	128	99

Age	All Persons	Males	Females
50-54	988	519	469
50	209	107	102
51	208	119	89
52	176	88	88
53	201	101	100
54	194	104	90
55-59	908	442	466
55	193	87	106
56	184	88	96
57	192	91	101
58	172	90	82
59	167	86	81
60-64	811	388	423
60	150	70	80
61	150	76	74
62	164	72	92
63	166	78	88
64	181	92	89
65-69	647	328	319
65	151	78	73
66	127	68	59
67	119	51	68
68	126	60	66
69	124	71	53
70-74	577	243	334
70	124	53	71
71	126	60	66
72	99	40	59
73	116	42	74
74	112	48	64
75-79	514	196	318
75	128	48	80
76	96	30	66
77	110	41	69
78	89	38	51
79	91	39	52
80-84	315	127	188
80	72	29	43
81	65	24	41
82	65	27	38
83	55	22	33
84	58	25	33
85-89	183	64	119
85	41	16	25
86	51	20	31
87	42	12	30
88	28	8	20
89	21	8	13
90 and over	72	7	65
Under 16	3776	1929	1847
Under 18	4315	2211	2104
16-44	6083	3020	3063
45-59/64*	3343	1917	1426
60/65** and over	2731	965	1766

* 45 – 64 for males; 45 – 59 for females.
** 65 and over for males; 60 and over for females.

Table P2

Population at Census Day 2001: Resident population by single year of age and sex

Age	All Persons	Males	Females	Age	All Persons	Males	Females
All ages	87058	43095	43963	50-54	4798	2388	2410
				50	956	453	503
0-4	6752	3445	3307	51	992	494	498
0	1219	631	588	52	1011	498	513
1	1336	681	655	53	918	476	442
2	1373	680	693	54	921	467	454
3	1427	759	668				
4	1397	694	703	55-59	4103	2024	2079
				55	870	421	449
5-9	7075	3679	3396	56	885	456	429
5	1420	768	652	57	844	415	429
6	1404	741	663	58	797	376	421
7	1360	703	657	59	707	356	351
8	1424	718	706				
9	1467	749	718	60-64	3511	1751	1760
				60	708	335	373
10-14	7771	4022	3749	61	753	399	354
10	1546	816	730	62	655	332	323
11	1533	805	728	63	667	331	336
12	1533	799	734	64	728	354	374
13	1588	797	791				
14	1571	805	766	65-69	3188	1509	1679
				65	712	345	367
15-19	7198	3651	3547	66	669	327	342
15	1531	755	776	67	630	295	335
16	1541	764	777	68	599	275	324
17	1557	784	773	69	578	267	311
18	1494	779	715				
19	1075	569	506	70-74	2637	1123	1514
				70	538	221	317
20-24	5618	2890	2728	71	565	255	310
20	1023	546	477	72	523	229	294
21	1155	600	555	73	485	204	281
22	1093	531	562	74	526	214	312
23	1153	596	557				
24	1194	617	577	75-79	2138	904	1234
				75	470	196	274
25-29	5771	2837	2934	76	444	186	258
25	1065	548	517	77	424	186	238
26	1094	568	526	78	418	185	233
27	1155	558	597	79	382	151	231
28	1175	579	596				
29	1282	584	698	80-84	1274	460	814
				80	334	113	221
30-34	6456	3184	3272	81	298	108	190
30	1332	675	657	82	238	91	147
31	1250	577	673	83	217	78	139
32	1289	633	656	84	187	70	117
33	1335	668	667				
34	1250	631	619	85-89	678	205	473
				85	198	77	121
35-39	6579	3335	3244	86	164	39	125
35	1348	699	649	87	122	41	81
36	1361	700	661	88	99	26	73
37	1362	675	687	89	95	22	73
38	1318	666	652				
39	1190	595	595	90 and over	271	54	217
40-44	6007	2993	3014	Under 16	23129	11901	11228
40	1327	671	656				
41	1210	576	634	Under 18	26227	13449	12778
42	1128	578	550				
43	1169	565	604	16-44	36098	18135	17963
44	1173	603	570				
				45-59/64*	15885	8804	7081
45-49	5233	2641	2592				
45	1060	538	522	60/65** and over	11946	4255	7691
46	1077	546	531				
47	1060	547	513				
48	1052	528	524				
49	984	482	502				

*   45 – 64 for males; 45 – 59 for females.
**   65 and over for males; 60 and over for females.

Table P2
Population at Census Day 2001: Resident population by single year of age and sex

Age	All Persons	Males	Females	Age	All Persons	Males	Females
All ages	79995	38661	41334	50-54	4893	2367	2526
				50	983	478	505
0-4	5107	2664	2443	51	929	455	474
0	985	529	456	52	986	481	505
1	959	482	477	53	974	484	490
2	1008	522	486	54	1021	469	552
3	1076	555	521				
4	1079	576	503	55-59	4504	2217	2287
				55	909	448	461
5-9	5484	2848	2636	56	927	448	479
5	1020	530	490	57	954	480	474
6	1104	592	512	58	903	453	450
7	1102	543	559	59	811	388	423
8	1109	570	539				
9	1149	613	536	60-64	3817	1804	2013
				60	735	367	368
10-14	5630	2884	2746	61	735	321	414
10	1156	579	577	62	822	404	418
11	1084	591	493	63	756	349	407
12	1124	547	577	64	769	363	406
13	1164	598	566				
14	1102	569	533	65-69	3401	1598	1803
				65	725	348	377
15-19	5536	2733	2803	66	692	334	358
15	1134	566	568	67	671	308	363
16	1143	563	580	68	626	292	334
17	1060	508	552	69	687	316	371
18	1003	507	496				
19	1196	589	607	70-74	3151	1402	1749
				70	674	301	373
20-24	4965	2425	2540	71	618	282	336
20	1009	512	497	72	630	282	348
21	982	493	489	73	622	261	361
22	994	497	497	74	607	276	331
23	991	466	525				
24	989	457	532	75-79	2360	956	1404
				75	559	227	332
25-29	5435	2626	2809	76	496	206	290
25	982	491	491	77	459	188	271
26	1085	498	587	78	418	167	251
27	1070	533	537	79	428	168	260
28	1126	561	565				
29	1172	543	629	80-84	1325	486	839
				80	360	139	221
30-34	6213	3018	3195	81	326	122	204
30	1268	633	635	82	241	93	148
31	1179	578	601	83	212	70	142
32	1249	609	640	84	186	62	124
33	1219	565	654				
34	1298	633	665	85-89	717	181	536
				85	191	55	136
35-39	6376	3114	3262	86	151	33	118
35	1269	644	625	87	154	31	123
36	1294	611	683	88	109	33	76
37	1325	625	700	89	112	29	83
38	1255	643	612				
39	1233	591	642	90 and over	331	64	267
40-44	5741	2760	2981	Under 16	17355	8962	8393
40	1216	567	649				
41	1148	545	603	Under 18	19558	10033	9525
42	1117	544	573				
43	1210	595	615	16-44	33132	16110	17022
44	1050	509	541				
				45-59/64*	16210	8902	7308
45-49	5009	2514	2495				
45	1070	551	519	60/65** and over	13298	4687	8611
46	971	490	481				
47	1016	524	492				
48	999	484	515				
49	953	465	488				

*   45 – 64 for males; 45 – 59 for females.
** 65 and over for males; 60 and over for females.

Table P2

Population at Census Day 2001: Resident population by single year of age and sex

Age	All Persons	Males	Females	Age	All Persons	Males	Females
All ages	76323	36821	39502	50-54	5481	2652	2829
				50	1035	507	528
0-4	4264	2192	2072	51	1046	522	524
0	797	410	387	52	1130	533	597
1	868	440	428	53	1143	535	608
2	856	437	419	54	1127	555	572
3	880	465	415				
4	863	440	423	55-59	4989	2442	2547
				55	1014	496	518
5-9	4659	2404	2255	56	1037	491	546
5	915	495	420	57	1138	566	572
6	883	449	434	58	953	463	490
7	938	498	440	59	847	426	421
8	895	438	457				
9	1028	524	504	60-64	3525	1701	1824
				60	709	345	364
10-14	5147	2600	2547	61	701	340	361
10	1083	580	503	62	725	343	382
11	932	451	481	63	698	337	361
12	1022	502	520	64	692	336	356
13	1029	531	498				
14	1081	536	545	65-69	3275	1518	1757
				65	705	337	368
15-19	5239	2745	2494	66	687	328	359
15	1083	564	519	67	606	277	329
16	1074	533	541	68	649	303	346
17	1135	596	539	69	628	273	355
18	1038	568	470				
19	909	484	425	70-74	2971	1281	1690
				70	610	280	330
20-24	4244	2212	2032	71	613	255	358
20	856	482	374	72	593	261	332
21	923	487	436	73	565	247	318
22	824	432	392	74	590	238	352
23	854	420	434				
24	787	391	396	75-79	2690	1026	1664
				75	589	227	362
25-29	4555	2351	2204	76	558	227	331
25	832	444	388	77	512	200	312
26	890	447	443	78	518	176	342
27	893	459	434	79	513	196	317
28	948	480	468				
29	992	521	471	80-84	1935	679	1256
				80	500	189	311
30-34	5393	2630	2763	81	463	174	289
30	1019	512	507	82	350	131	219
31	1102	540	562	83	308	92	216
32	1087	527	560	84	314	93	221
33	1081	524	557				
34	1104	527	577	85-89	1141	318	823
				85	271	75	196
35-39	5646	2731	2915	86	267	80	187
35	1056	510	546	87	227	62	165
36	1160	557	603	88	194	57	137
37	1147	560	587	89	182	44	138
38	1158	539	619				
39	1125	565	560	90 and over	522	130	392
40-44	5458	2619	2839	Under 16	15153	7760	7393
40	1138	538	600				
41	1082	540	542	Under 18	17362	8889	8473
42	1069	499	570				
43	1115	528	587	16-44	29452	14724	14728
44	1054	514	540				
				45-59/64*	17360	9385	7975
45-49	5189	2590	2599				
45	1041	532	509	60/65** and over	14358	4952	9406
46	995	490	505				
47	1063	532	531				
48	1041	500	541	* 45 – 64 for males; 45 – 59 for females.			
49	1049	536	513	** 65 and over for males; 60 and over for females.			

Table P2

Population at Census Day 2001: Resident population by single year of age and sex

Age	All Persons	Males	Females	Age	All Persons	Males	Females
All ages	47952	24038	23914	50-54	2626	1360	1266
				50	535	289	246
0-4	3615	1865	1750	51	566	294	272
0	712	363	349	52	536	265	271
1	716	368	348	53	487	246	241
2	713	368	345	54	502	266	236
3	735	387	348				
4	739	379	360	55-59	2239	1116	1123
				55	480	242	238
5-9	3822	1910	1912	56	468	227	241
5	783	403	380	57	460	238	222
6	758	376	382	58	438	227	211
7	803	398	405	59	393	182	211
8	733	366	367				
9	745	367	378	60-64	1866	901	965
				60	416	194	222
10-14	4082	2119	1963	61	394	186	208
10	777	414	363	62	387	190	197
11	814	414	400	63	327	172	155
12	784	410	374	64	342	159	183
13	848	444	404				
14	859	437	422	65-69	1637	811	826
				65	366	178	188
15-19	4102	2154	1948	66	296	166	130
15	880	435	445	67	334	155	179
16	879	461	418	68	318	158	160
17	929	467	462	69	323	154	169
18	827	447	380				
19	587	344	243	70-74	1388	623	765
				70	281	131	150
20-24	3182	1747	1435	71	289	130	159
20	621	372	249	72	259	102	157
21	626	356	270	73	275	117	158
22	639	336	303	74	284	143	141
23	690	380	310				
24	606	303	303	75-79	1142	464	678
				75	227	96	131
25-29	3449	1727	1722	76	247	109	138
25	612	334	278	77	232	98	134
26	671	314	357	78	237	88	149
27	683	350	333	79	199	73	126
28	756	355	401				
29	727	374	353	80-84	764	293	471
				80	190	80	110
30-34	3508	1778	1730	81	180	68	112
30	717	378	339	82	155	62	93
31	717	360	357	83	126	39	87
32	724	331	393	84	113	44	69
33	702	358	344				
34	648	351	297	85-89	440	142	298
				85	114	41	73
35-39	3493	1752	1741	86	114	40	74
35	688	343	345	87	85	34	51
36	712	346	366	88	72	18	54
37	677	328	349	89	55	9	46
38	759	406	353				
39	657	329	328	90 and over	162	42	120
40-44	3354	1634	1720	Under 16	12399	6329	6070
40	677	316	361				
41	692	339	353	Under 18	14207	7257	6950
42	669	336	333				
43	663	316	347	16-44	20208	10357	9851
44	653	327	326				
				45-59/64*	8847	4977	3870
45-49	3081	1600	1481				
45	682	373	309	60/65** and over	6498	2375	4123
46	623	319	304				
47	589	312	277				
48	617	316	301				
49	570	280	290				

*   45 – 64 for males; 45 – 59 for females.
**   65 and over for males; 60 and over for females.

Table P2

Population at Census Day 2001: Resident population by single year of age and sex

Age	All Persons	Males	Females	Age	All Persons	Males	Females
All ages	38248	19133	19115	50-54	2233	1121	1112
				50	456	251	205
0-4	3055	1580	1475	51	455	210	245
0	576	291	285	52	435	227	208
1	543	295	248	53	416	195	221
2	625	314	311	54	471	238	233
3	631	330	301				
4	680	350	330	55-59	1886	948	938
				55	399	209	190
5-9	2903	1479	1424	56	400	199	201
5	597	310	287	57	393	207	186
6	556	278	278	58	326	153	173
7	571	299	272	59	368	180	188
8	576	285	291				
9	603	307	296	60-64	1643	808	835
				60	325	156	169
10-14	3296	1682	1614	61	346	174	172
10	612	324	288	62	321	155	166
11	656	313	343	63	336	165	171
12	631	325	306	64	315	158	157
13	676	339	337				
14	721	381	340	65-69	1365	655	710
				65	281	146	135
15-19	3147	1605	1542	66	284	135	149
15	703	362	341	67	278	129	149
16	684	363	321	68	265	116	149
17	643	333	310	69	257	129	128
18	648	309	339				
19	469	238	231	70-74	1230	555	675
				70	260	128	132
20-24	2328	1202	1126	71	246	126	120
20	435	233	202	72	261	100	161
21	469	260	209	73	234	99	135
22	458	239	219	74	229	102	127
23	492	236	256				
24	474	234	240	75-79	877	371	506
				75	207	99	108
25-29	2860	1452	1408	76	204	97	107
25	471	244	227	77	170	59	111
26	500	254	246	78	154	62	92
27	529	251	278	79	142	54	88
28	673	373	300				
29	687	330	357	80-84	564	228	336
				80	129	58	71
30-34	2928	1445	1483	81	151	61	90
30	556	250	306	82	118	46	72
31	597	283	314	83	90	36	54
32	548	268	280	84	76	27	49
33	621	332	289				
34	606	312	294	85-89	288	97	191
				85	61	25	36
35-39	2923	1519	1404	86	70	29	41
35	623	335	288	87	60	21	39
36	640	310	330	88	57	13	44
37	587	331	256	89	40	9	31
38	533	257	276				
39	540	286	254	90 and over	115	35	80
40-44	2420	1218	1202	Under 16	9957	5103	4854
40	508	285	223				
41	487	253	234	Under 18	11284	5799	5485
42	479	227	252				
43	479	232	247	16-44	15903	8079	7824
44	467	221	246				
				45-59/64*	7114	4010	3104
45-49	2187	1133	1054				
45	444	224	220	60/65** and over	5274	1941	3333
46	439	225	214				
47	465	263	202				
48	440	214	226				
49	399	207	192				

*   45 – 64 for males; 45 – 59 for females.
**   65 and over for males; 60 and over for females.

Table P3

Population at Census Day 2001: Resident population by single year of age and sex

Age	All Persons	Males	Females		Age	All Persons	Males	Females
All ages	665968	318628	347340		50-54	38981	18964	20017
					50	7559	3751	3808
0-4	42128	21663	20465		51	7706	3754	3952
0	8030	4073	3957		52	7716	3744	3972
1	8050	4194	3856		53	7990	3873	4117
2	8467	4361	4106		54	8010	3842	4168
3	8599	4469	4130					
4	8982	4566	4416		55-59	35991	17540	18451
					55	7234	3591	3643
5-9	46450	23803	22647		56	7335	3560	3775
5	8833	4597	4236		57	7501	3600	3901
6	8966	4549	4417		58	7431	3591	3840
7	9154	4614	4540		59	6490	3198	3292
8	9504	4828	4676					
9	9993	5215	4778		60-64	29580	14026	15554
					60	5822	2789	3033
10-14	49357	25143	24214		61	5894	2808	3086
10	9841	5008	4833		62	6079	2862	3217
11	9656	4882	4774		63	5831	2769	3062
12	9878	5016	4862		64	5954	2798	3156
13	10000	5121	4879					
14	9982	5116	4866		65-69	27291	12369	14922
					65	5724	2611	3113
15-19	49746	24979	24767		66	5490	2574	2916
15	10052	5105	4947		67	5340	2462	2878
16	10112	5146	4966		68	5414	2354	3060
17	9602	4888	4714		69	5323	2368	2955
18	9642	4966	4676					
19	10338	4874	5464		70-74	25011	10534	14477
					70	5346	2312	3034
20-24	45050	22181	22869		71	5209	2174	3035
20	9840	4872	4968		72	4895	2081	2814
21	9501	4815	4686		73	4760	1995	2765
22	8887	4301	4586		74	4801	1972	2829
23	8452	4099	4353					
24	8370	4094	4276		75-79	20394	7896	12498
					75	4593	1822	2771
25-29	44298	21667	22631		76	4292	1744	2548
25	8662	4293	4369		77	4001	1539	2462
26	8533	4180	4353		78	3780	1418	2362
27	8832	4247	4585		79	3728	1373	2355
28	9227	4434	4793					
29	9044	4513	4531		80-84	13577	4832	8745
					80	3620	1362	2258
30-34	49415	23583	25832		81	3358	1266	2092
30	9657	4599	5058		82	2471	894	1577
31	9540	4565	4975		83	2124	674	1450
32	9885	4680	5205		84	2004	636	1368
33	9993	4817	5176					
34	10340	4922	5418		85-89	7373	2100	5273
					85	1825	541	1284
35-39	51137	24376	26761		86	1747	511	1236
35	10162	4919	5243		87	1481	437	1044
36	10541	5047	5494		88	1308	350	958
37	10272	4884	5388		89	1012	261	751
38	10129	4826	5303					
39	10033	4700	5333		90 and over	3478	731	2747
40-44	46722	22360	24362		Under 16	147987	75714	72273
40	9927	4750	5177					
41	9534	4613	4921		Under 18	167701	85748	81953
42	9201	4313	4888					
43	9303	4509	4794		16-44	276316	134041	142275
44	8757	4175	4582					
					45-59/64*	128987	70411	58576
45-49	39989	19881	20108					
45	8516	4234	4282		60/65** and over	112678	38462	74216
46	7931	3937	3994					
47	8066	4037	4029					
48	7897	3870	4027					
49	7579	3803	3776					

*   45 – 64 for males; 45 – 59 for females.
** 65 and over for males; 60 and over for females.

Table P3

Population at Census Day 2001: Resident population by single year of age and sex

Age	All Persons	Males	Females	Age	All Persons	Males	Females
All ages	426965	209098	217867	50-54	25755	12743	13012
				50	5153	2614	2539
0-4	28971	14907	14064	51	5142	2549	2593
0	5431	2845	2586	52	4994	2446	2548
1	5700	2922	2778	53	5087	2506	2581
2	5827	2991	2836	54	5379	2628	2751
3	5909	3024	2885				
4	6104	3125	2979	55-59	23603	11602	12001
				55	4790	2381	2409
5-9	30390	15538	14852	56	4766	2325	2441
5	5899	3044	2855	57	4920	2451	2469
6	6020	3109	2911	58	4807	2387	2420
7	6076	3049	3027	59	4320	2058	2262
8	6136	3139	2997				
9	6259	3197	3062	60-64	19614	9393	10221
				60	3963	1948	2015
10-14	32592	16725	15867	61	4015	1881	2134
10	6396	3243	3153	62	3987	1924	2063
11	6419	3298	3121	63	3820	1834	1986
12	6479	3330	3149	64	3829	1806	2023
13	6645	3409	3236				
14	6653	3445	3208	65-69	16909	8041	8868
				65	3574	1728	1846
15-19	31026	15712	15314	66	3468	1647	1821
15	6657	3418	3239	67	3370	1611	1759
16	6607	3433	3174	68	3303	1550	1753
17	6261	3099	3162	69	3194	1505	1689
18	6056	3052	3004				
19	5445	2710	2735	70-74	14738	6530	8208
				70	3263	1443	1820
20-24	26501	13228	13273	71	3059	1395	1664
20	5558	2814	2744	72	2880	1300	1580
21	5339	2634	2705	73	2711	1145	1566
22	5319	2686	2633	74	2825	1247	1578
23	5125	2507	2618				
24	5160	2587	2573	75-79	11764	4847	6917
				75	2641	1109	1532
25-29	28945	14348	14597	76	2426	1072	1354
25	5260	2610	2650	77	2351	977	1374
26	5392	2580	2812	78	2198	840	1358
27	5848	3032	2816	79	2148	849	1299
28	6072	2998	3074				
29	6373	3128	3245	80-84	7583	2838	4745
				80	1934	770	1164
30-34	33124	16414	16710	81	1797	670	1127
30	6672	3353	3319	82	1488	537	951
31	6489	3218	3271	83	1250	456	794
32	6639	3310	3329	84	1114	405	709
33	6650	3223	3427				
34	6674	3310	3364	85-89	3907	1102	2805
				85	962	295	667
35-39	33246	16375	16871	86	908	261	647
35	6734	3357	3377	87	818	218	600
36	6910	3358	3552	88	666	196	470
37	6855	3383	3472	89	553	132	421
38	6504	3279	3225				
39	6243	2998	3245	90 and over	1740	392	1348
40-44	29951	14845	15106	Under 16	98610	50588	48022
40	6241	3105	3136				
41	6109	2983	3126	Under 18	111478	57120	54358
42	5946	3039	2907				
43	5923	2879	3044	16-44	176136	87504	88632
44	5732	2839	2893				
				45-59/64*	85357	47256	38101
45-49	26606	13518	13088				
45	5625	2788	2837	60/65** and over	66862	23750	43112
46	5287	2715	2572				
47	5273	2759	2514				
48	5303	2673	2630				
49	5118	2583	2535				

*   45 – 64 for males; 45 – 59 for females.
** 65 and over for males; 60 and over for females.

Table P3

Population at Census Day 2001: Resident population by single year of age and sex

Age	All Persons	Males	Females	Age	All Persons	Males	Females
All ages	311119	154100	157019	50-54	17765	8751	9014
				50	3491	1731	1760
0-4	23018	11803	11215	51	3610	1787	1823
0	4249	2193	2056	52	3618	1825	1793
1	4607	2344	2263	53	3550	1711	1839
2	4659	2350	2309	54	3496	1697	1799
3	4745	2487	2258				
4	4758	2429	2329	55-59	15763	7807	7956
				55	3292	1622	1670
5-9	24253	12594	11659	56	3304	1640	1664
5	4714	2478	2236	57	3177	1590	1587
6	4790	2546	2244	58	3170	1560	1610
7	4799	2455	2344	59	2820	1395	1425
8	4867	2493	2374				
9	5083	2622	2461	60-64	13192	6406	6786
				60	2698	1316	1382
10-14	26228	13587	12641	61	2676	1344	1332
10	5216	2748	2468	62	2644	1253	1391
11	5140	2682	2458	63	2544	1237	1307
12	5210	2743	2467	64	2630	1256	1374
13	5296	2642	2654				
14	5366	2772	2594	65-69	11667	5478	6189
				65	2550	1248	1302
15-19	24408	12481	11927	66	2341	1108	1233
15	5251	2708	2543	67	2326	1063	1263
16	5380	2662	2718	68	2254	1027	1227
17	5214	2654	2560	69	2196	1032	1164
18	4899	2527	2372				
19	3664	1930	1734	70-74	9889	4301	5588
				70	2145	916	1229
20-24	19138	9784	9354	71	2085	941	1144
20	3659	1976	1683	72	1946	867	1079
21	3876	2012	1864	73	1909	807	1102
22	3808	1903	1905	74	1804	770	1034
23	3819	1928	1891				
24	3976	1965	2011	75-79	7931	3239	4692
				75	1801	765	1036
25-29	21189	10544	10645	76	1693	685	1008
25	3940	1998	1942	77	1576	668	908
26	3909	2004	1905	78	1505	604	901
27	4255	2108	2147	79	1356	517	839
28	4412	2224	2188				
29	4673	2210	2463	80-84	5009	1842	3167
				80	1301	476	825
30-34	23688	11925	11763	81	1162	435	727
30	4712	2398	2314	82	1011	386	625
31	4659	2374	2285	83	790	283	507
32	4727	2337	2390	84	745	262	483
33	4815	2439	2376				
34	4775	2377	2398	85-89	2605	808	1797
				85	727	241	486
35-39	23922	12040	11882	86	618	192	426
35	4822	2452	2370	87	495	157	338
36	4936	2484	2452	88	427	135	292
37	4887	2449	2438	89	338	83	255
38	4703	2370	2333				
39	4574	2285	2289	90 and over	1081	242	839
40-44	21659	10871	10788	Under 16	78750	40692	38058
40	4594	2328	2266				
41	4536	2237	2299	Under 18	89344	46008	43336
42	4165	2088	2077				
43	4266	2143	2123	16-44	128753	64937	63816
44	4098	2075	2023				
45-49	18714	9597	9117	45-59/64*	58648	32561	26087
45	3946	2002	1944				
46	3802	1994	1808	60/65** and over	44968	15910	29058
47	3745	1908	1837				
48	3769	1970	1799				
49	3452	1723	1729				

*   45 – 64 for males; 45 – 59 for females.
**   65 and over for males; 60 and over for females.

Table P3

Population at Census Day 2001: Resident population by single year of age and sex

Age	All Persons	Males	Females	Age	All Persons	Males	Females
All ages	281215	139623	141592	50-54	15925	8026	7899
				50	3271	1669	1602
0-4	21121	10840	10281	51	3239	1631	1608
0	3973	2005	1968	52	3221	1626	1595
1	4006	2090	1916	53	3026	1488	1538
2	4311	2185	2126	54	3168	1612	1556
3	4331	2217	2114				
4	4500	2343	2157	55-59	13375	6636	6739
				55	2806	1431	1375
5-9	21957	11212	10745	56	2756	1348	1408
5	4437	2302	2135	57	2829	1440	1389
6	4288	2176	2112	58	2607	1245	1362
7	4371	2252	2119	59	2377	1172	1205
8	4400	2216	2184				
9	4461	2266	2195	60-64	11201	5576	5625
				60	2298	1136	1162
10-14	24487	12559	11928	61	2236	1120	1116
10	4736	2437	2299	62	2289	1139	1150
11	4748	2409	2339	63	2191	1123	1068
12	4836	2472	2364	64	2187	1058	1129
13	5056	2617	2439				
14	5111	2624	2487	65-69	9474	4518	4956
				65	2028	967	1061
15-19	24021	12426	11595	66	1900	940	960
15	5144	2656	2488	67	1893	875	1018
16	5083	2616	2467	68	1819	853	966
17	5199	2662	2537	69	1834	883	951
18	4795	2453	2342				
19	3800	2039	1761	70-74	8214	3704	4510
				70	1723	819	904
20-24	18696	9720	8976	71	1646	765	881
20	3734	1986	1748	72	1694	716	978
21	3733	2017	1716	73	1558	671	887
22	3703	1895	1808	74	1593	733	860
23	3770	1908	1862				
24	3756	1914	1842	75-79	6453	2580	3873
				75	1451	621	830
25-29	20272	10069	10203	76	1350	557	793
25	3759	1898	1861	77	1317	528	789
26	3850	1891	1959	78	1240	462	778
27	3998	1979	2019	79	1095	412	683
28	4310	2138	2172				
29	4355	2163	2192	80-84	4120	1578	2542
				80	1038	428	610
30-34	21290	10565	10725	81	981	372	609
30	4234	2071	2163	82	851	340	511
31	4277	2100	2177	83	656	234	422
32	4281	2098	2183	84	594	204	390
33	4323	2178	2145				
34	4175	2118	2057	85-89	2231	697	1534
				85	572	193	379
35-39	21334	10639	10695	86	513	176	337
35	4402	2159	2243	87	454	140	314
36	4458	2230	2228	88	389	108	281
37	4184	2104	2080	89	303	80	223
38	4242	2116	2126				
39	4048	2030	2018	90 and over	886	232	654
40-44	19003	9356	9647	Under 16	72709	37267	35442
40	4085	2026	2059				
41	3895	1941	1954	Under 18	82991	42545	40446
42	3727	1791	1936				
43	3725	1822	1903	16-44	119472	60119	59353
44	3571	1776	1795				
45-49	17155	8690	8465	45-59/64*	52031	28928	23103
45	3633	1871	1762				
46	3562	1848	1714	60/65** and over	37003	13309	23694
47	3429	1730	1699				
48	3329	1666	1663				
49	3202	1575	1627				

*   45 – 64 for males; 45 – 59 for females.
** 65 and over for males; 60 and over for females.

Table P4

Population at Census Day 2001: Resident population by single year of age and sex

Age	All Persons	Males	Females	Age	All Persons	Males	Females
All ages	277391	129778	147613	50-54	14223	6845	7378
				50	2845	1390	1455
0-4	16616	8465	8151	51	2797	1324	1473
0	3293	1632	1661	52	2720	1326	1394
1	3090	1648	1442	53	2885	1409	1476
2	3292	1697	1595	54	2976	1396	1580
3	3337	1707	1630				
4	3604	1781	1823	55-59	13631	6526	7105
				55	2698	1327	1371
5-9	18722	9512	9210	56	2716	1305	1411
5	3388	1741	1647	57	2804	1326	1478
6	3564	1767	1797	58	2890	1363	1527
7	3764	1863	1901	59	2523	1205	1318
8	3939	2005	1934				
9	4067	2136	1931	60-64	12149	5693	6456
				60	2257	1096	1161
10-14	20588	10478	10110	61	2420	1141	1279
10	3973	2025	1948	62	2468	1132	1336
11	3931	1966	1965	63	2483	1160	1323
12	4166	2138	2028	64	2521	1164	1357
13	4276	2133	2143				
14	4242	2216	2026	65-69	11723	5153	6570
				65	2430	1054	1376
15-19	22650	11040	11610	66	2314	1028	1286
15	4335	2191	2144	67	2327	1046	1281
16	4296	2206	2090	68	2303	984	1319
17	4006	2048	1958	69	2349	1041	1308
18	4261	2155	2106				
19	5752	2440	3312	70-74	11035	4458	6577
				70	2384	948	1436
20-24	23261	11038	12223	71	2328	951	1377
20	5290	2409	2881	72	2104	865	1239
21	5039	2386	2653	73	2106	854	1252
22	4595	2188	2407	74	2113	840	1273
23	4191	2006	2185				
24	4146	2049	2097	75-79	8964	3325	5639
				75	2018	796	1222
25-29	20152	9580	10572	76	1929	760	1169
25	4229	2011	2218	77	1750	606	1144
26	4063	1945	2118	78	1648	600	1048
27	4043	1860	2183	79	1619	563	1056
28	4105	1976	2129				
29	3712	1788	1924	80-84	5847	1971	3876
				80	1578	561	1017
30-34	19652	9183	10469	81	1463	532	931
30	3990	1875	2115	82	1074	368	706
31	3893	1860	2033	83	884	255	629
32	3854	1762	2092	84	848	255	593
33	3851	1831	2020				
34	4064	1855	2209	85-89	3277	903	2374
				85	801	239	562
35-39	19825	9280	10545	86	800	236	564
35	3961	1873	2088	87	671	184	487
36	4053	1927	2126	88	564	134	430
37	4057	1908	2149	89	441	110	331
38	3871	1784	2087				
39	3883	1788	2095	90 and over	1523	295	1228
40-44	18366	8534	9832	Under 16	60261	30646	29615
40	3879	1821	2058				
41	3706	1740	1966	Under 18	68563	34900	33663
42	3638	1634	2004				
43	3649	1747	1902	16-44	119571	56464	63107
44	3494	1592	1902				
				45-59/64*	48734	26563	22171
45-49	15187	7499	7688				
45	3229	1565	1664	60/65** and over	48825	16105	32720
46	3047	1501	1546				
47	3064	1505	1559				
48	3032	1485	1547				
49	2815	1443	1372				

*   45 – 64 for males; 45 – 59 for females.
** 65 and over for males; 60 and over for females.

Table P4

Population at Census Day 2001: Resident population by single year of age and sex

Age	All Persons	Males	Females
All ages	394384	192910	201474
0-4	26608	13680	12928
0	5017	2613	2404
1	5215	2685	2530
2	5348	2753	2595
3	5441	2770	2671
4	5587	2859	2728
5-9	27818	14233	13585
5	5405	2771	2634
6	5496	2843	2653
7	5579	2801	2778
8	5615	2884	2731
9	5723	2934	2789
10-14	29679	15235	14444
10	5820	2949	2871
11	5837	2999	2838
12	5895	3031	2864
13	6063	3113	2950
14	6064	3143	2921
15-19	28272	14302	13970
15	6050	3097	2953
16	5968	3101	2867
17	5672	2813	2859
18	5513	2781	2732
19	5069	2510	2559
20-24	24293	12060	12233
20	5092	2570	2522
21	4893	2405	2488
22	4896	2460	2436
23	4684	2275	2409
24	4728	2350	2378
25-29	26610	13183	13427
25	4778	2376	2402
26	4965	2372	2593
27	5389	2793	2596
28	5590	2758	2832
29	5888	2884	3004
30-34	30807	15274	15533
30	6166	3100	3066
31	6031	2981	3050
32	6210	3104	3106
33	6171	2989	3182
34	6229	3100	3129
35-39	30871	15187	15684
35	6256	3135	3121
36	6415	3106	3309
37	6353	3128	3225
38	6040	3017	3023
39	5807	2801	3006
40-44	27724	13735	13989
40	5788	2886	2902
41	5635	2757	2878
42	5527	2794	2733
43	5482	2684	2798
44	5292	2614	2678
45-49	24672	12546	12126
45	5221	2590	2631
46	4899	2514	2385
47	4899	2573	2326
48	4908	2457	2451
49	4745	2412	2333

Age	All Persons	Males	Females
50-54	23906	11826	12080
50	4766	2421	2345
51	4783	2371	2412
52	4637	2278	2359
53	4713	2323	2390
54	5007	2433	2574
55-59	21938	10778	11160
55	4441	2221	2220
56	4414	2149	2265
57	4569	2270	2299
58	4486	2221	2265
59	4028	1917	2111
60-64	18290	8750	9540
60	3676	1790	1886
61	3724	1747	1977
62	3730	1804	1926
63	3565	1713	1852
64	3595	1696	1899
65-69	15846	7532	8314
65	3338	1611	1727
66	3253	1533	1720
67	3154	1508	1646
68	3101	1456	1645
69	3000	1424	1576
70-74	13765	6064	7701
70	3078	1344	1734
71	2839	1286	1553
72	2672	1209	1463
73	2542	1064	1478
74	2634	1161	1473
75-79	10960	4500	6460
75	2476	1032	1444
76	2257	994	1263
77	2169	893	1276
78	2068	795	1273
79	1990	786	1204
80-84	7055	2647	4408
80	1800	716	1084
81	1663	624	1039
82	1380	492	888
83	1175	434	741
84	1037	381	656
85-89	3640	1021	2619
85	895	274	621
86	840	242	598
87	770	200	570
88	607	179	428
89	528	126	402
90 and over	1630	357	1273
Under 16	90155	46245	43910
Under 18	101795	52159	49636
16-44	162527	80644	81883
45-59/64*	79266	43900	35366
60/65** and over	62436	22121	40315

* 45 – 64 for males; 45 – 59 for females.
** 65 and over for males; 60 and over for females.

Table P4

Population at Census Day 2001: Resident population by single year of age and sex

Age	All Persons	Males	Females	Age	All Persons	Males	Females
All ages	388577	188850	199727	50-54	24758	12119	12639
				50	4714	2361	2353
0-4	25512	13198	12314	51	4909	2430	2479
0	4737	2441	2296	52	4996	2418	2578
1	4960	2546	2414	53	5105	2464	2641
2	5175	2664	2511	54	5034	2446	2588
3	5262	2762	2500				
4	5378	2785	2593	55-59	22360	11014	11346
				55	4536	2264	2272
5-9	27728	14291	13437	56	4619	2255	2364
5	5445	2856	2589	57	4697	2274	2423
6	5402	2782	2620	58	4541	2228	2313
7	5390	2751	2639	59	3967	1993	1974
8	5565	2823	2742				
9	5926	3079	2847	60-64	17431	8333	9098
				60	3565	1693	1872
10-14	28769	14665	14104	61	3474	1667	1807
10	5868	2983	2885	62	3611	1730	1881
11	5725	2916	2809	63	3348	1609	1739
12	5712	2878	2834	64	3433	1634	1799
13	5724	2988	2736				
14	5740	2900	2840	65-69	15568	7216	8352
				65	3294	1557	1737
15-19	27096	13939	13157	66	3176	1546	1630
15	5717	2914	2803	67	3013	1416	1597
16	5816	2940	2876	68	3111	1370	1741
17	5596	2840	2756	69	2974	1327	1647
18	5381	2811	2570				
19	4586	2434	2152	70-74	13976	6076	7900
				70	2962	1364	1598
20-24	21789	11143	10646	71	2881	1223	1658
20	4550	2463	2087	72	2791	1216	1575
21	4462	2429	2033	73	2654	1141	1513
22	4292	2113	2179	74	2688	1132	1556
23	4261	2093	2168				
24	4224	2045	2179	75-79	11430	4571	6859
				75	2575	1026	1549
25-29	24146	12087	12059	76	2363	984	1379
25	4433	2282	2151	77	2251	933	1318
26	4470	2235	2235	78	2132	818	1314
27	4789	2387	2402	79	2109	810	1299
28	5122	2458	2664				
29	5332	2725	2607	80-84	7730	2861	4869
				80	2042	801	1241
30-34	29763	14400	15363	81	1895	734	1161
30	5667	2724	2943	82	1397	526	871
31	5647	2705	2942	83	1240	419	821
32	6031	2918	3113	84	1156	381	775
33	6142	2986	3156				
34	6276	3067	3209	85-89	4096	1197	2899
				85	1024	302	722
35-39	31312	15096	16216	86	947	275	672
35	6201	3046	3155	87	810	253	557
36	6488	3120	3368	88	744	216	528
37	6215	2976	3239	89	571	151	420
38	6258	3042	3216				
39	6150	2912	3238	90 and over	1955	436	1519
40-44	28356	13826	14530	Under 16	87726	45068	42658
40	6048	2929	3119				
41	5828	2873	2955	Under 18	99138	50848	48290
42	5563	2679	2884				
43	5654	2762	2892	16-44	156745	77577	79168
44	5263	2583	2680				
				45-59/64*	80253	43848	36405
45-49	24802	12382	12420				
45	5287	2669	2618	60/65** and over	63853	22357	41496
46	4884	2436	2448				
47	5002	2532	2470				
48	4865	2385	2480				
49	4764	2360	2404				

*   45 – 64 for males; 45 – 59 for females.
** 65 and over for males; 60 and over for females.

Table P4

Population at Census Day 2001: Resident population by single year of age and sex

Age	All Persons	Males	Females	Age	All Persons	Males	Females
All ages	343700	170288	173412	50-54	19614	9668	9946
				50	3878	1924	1954
0-4	25381	13030	12351	51	3969	1965	2004
0	4663	2425	2238	52	3975	1993	1982
1	5092	2581	2511	53	3924	1894	2030
2	5138	2588	2550	54	3868	1892	1976
3	5213	2741	2472				
4	5275	2695	2580	55-59	17428	8631	8797
				55	3641	1782	1859
5-9	26825	13899	12926	56	3656	1816	1840
5	5208	2751	2457	57	3528	1771	1757
6	5314	2812	2502	58	3491	1726	1765
7	5296	2703	2593	59	3112	1536	1576
8	5388	2748	2640				
9	5619	2885	2734	60-64	14516	7049	7467
				60	2985	1474	1511
10-14	29141	15077	14064	61	2967	1478	1489
10	5792	3042	2750	62	2901	1373	1528
11	5722	2981	2741	63	2799	1358	1441
12	5794	3042	2752	64	2864	1366	1498
13	5878	2938	2940				
14	5955	3074	2881	65-69	12730	5987	6743
				65	2786	1365	1421
15-19	27162	13891	13271	66	2556	1222	1334
15	5858	3029	2829	67	2542	1166	1376
16	6019	2994	3025	68	2456	1121	1335
17	5803	2940	2863	69	2390	1113	1277
18	5442	2798	2644				
19	4040	2130	1910	70-74	10862	4767	6095
				70	2330	1015	1315
20-24	21346	10952	10394	71	2305	1050	1255
20	4125	2220	1905	72	2154	958	1196
21	4322	2241	2081	73	2078	888	1190
22	4231	2129	2102	74	1995	856	1139
23	4260	2160	2100				
24	4408	2202	2206	75-79	8735	3586	5149
				75	1966	842	1124
25-29	23524	11709	11815	76	1862	763	1099
25	4422	2232	2190	77	1758	752	1006
26	4336	2212	2124	78	1635	649	986
27	4714	2347	2367	79	1514	580	934
28	4894	2464	2430				
29	5158	2454	2704	80-84	5537	2033	3504
				80	1435	530	905
30-34	26005	13065	12940	81	1296	481	815
30	5218	2651	2567	82	1119	431	688
31	5117	2611	2506	83	865	305	560
32	5156	2543	2613	84	822	286	536
33	5294	2673	2621				
34	5220	2587	2633	85-89	2872	889	1983
				85	794	262	532
35-39	26297	13228	13069	86	686	211	475
35	5300	2674	2626	87	543	175	368
36	5431	2736	2695	88	486	152	334
37	5389	2704	2685	89	363	89	274
38	5167	2632	2535				
39	5010	2482	2528	90 and over	1191	277	914
40-44	23886	11981	11905	Under 16	87205	45035	42170
40	5047	2547	2500				
41	5010	2463	2547	Under 18	99027	50969	48058
42	4584	2333	2251				
43	4707	2338	2369	16-44	142362	71797	70565
44	4538	2300	2238				
				45-59/64*	64739	35917	28822
45-49	20648	10569	10079				
45	4350	2200	2150	60/65** and over	49394	17539	31855
46	4190	2195	1995				
47	4119	2094	2025				
48	4164	2186	1978				
49	3825	1894	1931				

*   45 – 64 for males; 45 – 59 for females.
** 65 and over for males; 60 and over for females.

CENSUS

Table P4

Population at Census Day 2001: Resident population by single year of age and sex

Age	All Persons	Males	Females	Age	All Persons	Males	Females
All ages	281215	139623	141592	50-54	15925	8026	7899
				50	3271	1669	1602
0-4	21121	10840	10281	51	3239	1631	1608
0	3973	2005	1968	52	3221	1626	1595
1	4006	2090	1916	53	3026	1488	1538
2	4311	2185	2126	54	3168	1612	1556
3	4331	2217	2114				
4	4500	2343	2157	55-59	13375	6636	6739
				55	2806	1431	1375
5-9	21957	11212	10745	56	2756	1348	1408
5	4437	2302	2135	57	2829	1440	1389
6	4288	2176	2112	58	2607	1245	1362
7	4371	2252	2119	59	2377	1172	1205
8	4400	2216	2184				
9	4461	2266	2195	60-64	11201	5576	5625
				60	2298	1136	1162
10-14	24487	12559	11928	61	2236	1120	1116
10	4736	2437	2299	62	2289	1139	1150
11	4748	2409	2339	63	2191	1123	1068
12	4836	2472	2364	64	2187	1058	1129
13	5056	2617	2439				
14	5111	2624	2487	65-69	9474	4518	4956
				65	2028	967	1061
15-19	24021	12426	11595	66	1900	940	960
15	5144	2656	2488	67	1893	875	1018
16	5083	2616	2467	68	1819	853	966
17	5199	2662	2537	69	1834	883	951
18	4795	2453	2342				
19	3800	2039	1761	70-74	8214	3704	4510
				70	1723	819	904
20-24	18696	9720	8976	71	1646	765	881
20	3734	1986	1748	72	1694	716	978
21	3733	2017	1716	73	1558	671	887
22	3703	1895	1808	74	1593	733	860
23	3770	1908	1862				
24	3756	1914	1842	75-79	6453	2580	3873
				75	1451	621	830
25-29	20272	10069	10203	76	1350	557	793
25	3759	1898	1861	77	1317	528	789
26	3850	1891	1959	78	1240	462	778
27	3998	1979	2019	79	1095	412	683
28	4310	2138	2172				
29	4355	2163	2192	80-84	4120	1578	2542
				80	1038	428	610
30-34	21290	10565	10725	81	981	372	609
30	4234	2071	2163	82	851	340	511
31	4277	2100	2177	83	656	234	422
32	4281	2098	2183	84	594	204	390
33	4323	2178	2145				
34	4175	2118	2057	85-89	2231	697	1534
				85	572	193	379
35-39	21334	10639	10695	86	513	176	337
35	4402	2159	2243	87	454	140	314
36	4458	2230	2228	88	389	108	281
37	4184	2104	2080	89	303	80	223
38	4242	2116	2126				
39	4048	2030	2018	90 and over	886	232	654
40-44	19003	9356	9647	Under 16	72709	37267	35442
40	4085	2026	2059				
41	3895	1941	1954	Under 18	82991	42545	40446
42	3727	1791	1936				
43	3725	1822	1903	16-44	119472	60119	59353
44	3571	1776	1795				
				45-59/64*	52031	28928	23103
45-49	17155	8690	8465				
45	3633	1871	1762	60/65** and over	37003	13309	23694
46	3562	1848	1714				
47	3429	1730	1699				
48	3329	1666	1663				
49	3202	1575	1627				

*   45 – 64 for males; 45 – 59 for females.
**   65 and over for males; 60 and over for females.

Table P5

Population at Census Day 2001: Resident population by single year of age and sex

Age	All Persons	Males	Females	Age	All Persons	Males	Females
All ages	277391	129778	147613	50-54	14223	6845	7378
				50	2845	1390	1455
0-4	16616	8465	8151	51	2797	1324	1473
0	3293	1632	1661	52	2720	1326	1394
1	3090	1648	1442	53	2885	1409	1476
2	3292	1697	1595	54	2976	1396	1580
3	3337	1707	1630				
4	3604	1781	1823	55-59	13631	6526	7105
				55	2698	1327	1371
5-9	18722	9512	9210	56	2716	1305	1411
5	3388	1741	1647	57	2804	1326	1478
6	3564	1767	1797	58	2890	1363	1527
7	3764	1863	1901	59	2523	1205	1318
8	3939	2005	1934				
9	4067	2136	1931	60-64	12149	5693	6456
				60	2257	1096	1161
10-14	20588	10478	10110	61	2420	1141	1279
10	3973	2025	1948	62	2468	1132	1336
11	3931	1966	1965	63	2483	1160	1323
12	4166	2138	2028	64	2521	1164	1357
13	4276	2133	2143				
14	4242	2216	2026	65-69	11723	5153	6570
				65	2430	1054	1376
15-19	22650	11040	11610	66	2314	1028	1286
15	4335	2191	2144	67	2327	1046	1281
16	4296	2206	2090	68	2303	984	1319
17	4006	2048	1958	69	2349	1041	1308
18	4261	2155	2106				
19	5752	2440	3312	70-74	11035	4458	6577
				70	2384	948	1436
20-24	23261	11038	12223	71	2328	951	1377
20	5290	2409	2881	72	2104	865	1239
21	5039	2386	2653	73	2106	854	1252
22	4595	2188	2407	74	2113	840	1273
23	4191	2006	2185				
24	4146	2049	2097	75-79	8964	3325	5639
				75	2018	796	1222
25-29	20152	9580	10572	76	1929	760	1169
25	4229	2011	2218	77	1750	606	1144
26	4063	1945	2118	78	1648	600	1048
27	4043	1860	2183	79	1619	563	1056
28	4105	1976	2129				
29	3712	1788	1924	80-84	5847	1971	3876
				80	1578	561	1017
30-34	19652	9183	10469	81	1463	532	931
30	3990	1875	2115	82	1074	368	706
31	3893	1860	2033	83	884	255	629
32	3854	1762	2092	84	848	255	593
33	3851	1831	2020				
34	4064	1855	2209	85-89	3277	903	2374
				85	801	239	562
35-39	19825	9280	10545	86	800	236	564
35	3961	1873	2088	87	671	184	487
36	4053	1927	2126	88	564	134	430
37	4057	1908	2149	89	441	110	331
38	3871	1784	2087				
39	3883	1788	2095	90 and over	1523	295	1228
40-44	18366	8534	9832	Under 16	60261	30646	29615
40	3879	1821	2058				
41	3706	1740	1966	Under 18	68563	34900	33663
42	3638	1634	2004				
43	3649	1747	1902	16-44	119571	56464	63107
44	3494	1592	1902				
				45-59/64*	48734	26563	22171
45-49	15187	7499	7688				
45	3229	1565	1664	60/65** and over	48825	16105	32720
46	3047	1501	1546				
47	3064	1505	1559				
48	3032	1485	1547				
49	2815	1443	1372				

*   45 – 64 for males; 45 – 59 for females.
** 65 and over for males; 60 and over for females.

Table P5

Population at Census Day 2001: Resident population by single year of age and sex

Age	All Persons	Males	Females	Age	All Persons	Males	Females
All ages	369159	178369	190790	50-54	22800	11062	11738
				50	4418	2199	2219
0-4	23985	12469	11516	51	4450	2231	2219
0	4560	2408	2152	52	4585	2188	2397
1	4608	2346	2262	53	4608	2192	2416
2	4801	2461	2340	54	4739	2252	2487
3	4932	2578	2354				
4	5084	2676	2408	55-59	20876	10163	10713
				55	4150	2061	2089
5-9	26064	13481	12583	56	4307	2071	2236
5	5069	2651	2418	57	4461	2134	2327
6	5136	2676	2460	58	4222	2080	2142
7	5096	2601	2495	59	3736	1817	1919
8	5205	2656	2549				
9	5558	2897	2661	60-64	16725	7964	8761
				60	3363	1644	1719
10-14	26759	13577	13182	61	3334	1560	1774
10	5473	2738	2735	62	3476	1655	1821
11	5303	2718	2585	63	3242	1554	1688
12	5309	2646	2663	64	3310	1551	1759
13	5319	2762	2557				
14	5355	2713	2642	65-69	15219	7030	8189
				65	3237	1524	1713
15-19	25227	12844	12383	66	3054	1457	1597
15	5334	2712	2622	67	2960	1356	1604
16	5344	2697	2647	68	2982	1351	1631
17	5108	2547	2561	69	2986	1342	1644
18	4845	2539	2306				
19	4596	2349	2247	70-74	13802	6030	7772
				70	2963	1353	1610
20-24	20995	10517	10478	71	2805	1208	1597
20	4375	2343	2032	72	2760	1207	1553
21	4275	2267	2008	73	2601	1101	1500
22	4116	2019	2097	74	2673	1161	1512
23	4108	1946	2162				
24	4121	1942	2179	75-79	11081	4401	6680
				75	2502	996	1506
25-29	23402	11527	11875	76	2280	957	1323
25	4144	2074	2070	77	2220	901	1319
26	4452	2171	2281	78	2053	773	1280
27	4625	2288	2337	79	2026	774	1252
28	5000	2440	2560				
29	5181	2554	2627	80-84	7053	2552	4501
				80	1902	723	1179
30-34	28769	13826	14943	81	1736	672	1064
30	5516	2661	2855	82	1286	474	812
31	5550	2667	2883	83	1091	340	751
32	5789	2769	3020	84	1038	343	695
33	5824	2798	3026				
34	6090	2931	3159	85-89	3739	1045	2694
				85	977	269	708
35-39	30229	14598	15631	86	829	242	587
35	5965	2943	3022	87	751	208	543
36	6236	2969	3267	88	658	192	466
37	6142	2944	3198	89	524	134	390
38	6036	2933	3103				
39	5850	2809	3041	90 and over	1773	362	1411
40-44	27159	13111	14048	Under 16	82142	42239	39903
40	5851	2791	3060				
41	5539	2680	2859	Under 18	92594	47483	45111
42	5349	2580	2769				
43	5385	2641	2744	16-44	150447	73711	76736
44	5035	2419	2616				
				45-59/64*	75142	40999	34143
45-49	23502	11810	11692				
45	5014	2515	2499	60/65** and over	61428	21420	40008
46	4593	2309	2284				
47	4730	2426	2304				
48	4659	2272	2387	* 45 – 64 for males; 45 – 59 for females.			
49	4506	2288	2218	** 65 and over for males; 60 and over for females.			

Table P5

Population at Census Day 2001: Resident population by single year of age and sex

Age	All Persons	Males	Females	Age	All Persons	Males	Females
All ages	396943	195777	201166	50-54	24835	12274	12561
				50	4805	2431	2374
0-4	26992	13892	13100	51	5042	2469	2573
0	5020	2569	2451	52	4883	2460	2423
1	5317	2798	2519	53	5053	2450	2603
2	5455	2816	2639	54	5052	2464	2588
3	5532	2840	2692				
4	5668	2869	2799	55-59	22581	11215	11366
				55	4675	2308	2367
5-9	28833	14881	13952	56	4578	2296	2282
5	5594	2900	2694	57	4598	2306	2292
6	5638	2942	2696	58	4680	2306	2374
7	5779	2952	2827	59	4050	1999	2051
8	5841	2973	2868				
9	5981	3114	2867	60-64	17976	8641	9335
				60	3671	1767	1904
10-14	30400	15766	14634	61	3585	1712	1873
10	6025	3197	2828	62	3674	1785	1889
11	5961	3086	2875	63	3516	1690	1826
12	6033	3147	2886	64	3530	1687	1843
13	6297	3200	3097				
14	6084	3136	2948	65-69	15461	7298	8163
				65	3291	1606	1685
15-19	28544	14686	13858	66	3219	1525	1694
15	6125	3167	2958	67	3055	1447	1608
16	6160	3099	3061	68	3048	1385	1663
17	5922	3040	2882	69	2848	1335	1513
18	5750	2950	2800				
19	4587	2430	2157	70-74	13174	5824	7350
				70	2899	1297	1602
20-24	23027	11738	11289	71	2731	1219	1512
20	4718	2537	2181	72	2599	1170	1429
21	4667	2399	2268	73	2466	1080	1386
22	4585	2290	2295	74	2479	1058	1421
23	4532	2284	2248				
24	4525	2228	2297	75-79	10570	4293	6277
				75	2371	986	1385
25-29	26099	13216	12883	76	2223	937	1286
25	4805	2451	2354	77	2067	878	1189
26	4811	2397	2414	78	2011	776	1235
27	5203	2668	2535	79	1898	716	1182
28	5464	2752	2712				
29	5816	2948	2868	80-84	7191	2737	4454
				80	1847	751	1096
30-34	31256	15594	15662	81	1695	634	1061
30	6022	2962	3060	82	1421	527	894
31	6059	3037	3022	83	1178	438	740
32	6358	3224	3134	84	1050	387	663
33	6365	3135	3230				
34	6452	3236	3216	85-89	3765	1125	2640
				85	951	314	637
35-39	31558	15596	15962	86	904	257	647
35	6394	3206	3188	87	734	233	501
36	6593	3235	3358	88	650	197	453
37	6325	3133	3192	89	526	124	402
38	6253	3135	3118				
39	5993	2887	3106	90 and over	1739	399	1340
40-44	28049	14030	14019	Under 16	92350	47706	44644
40	5771	2924	2847				
41	5862	2925	2937	Under 18	104432	53845	50587
42	5549	2769	2780				
43	5623	2780	2843	16-44	162408	81693	80715
44	5244	2632	2612				
				45-59/64*	80950	44702	36248
45-49	24893	12572	12321				
45	5279	2654	2625	60/65** and over	61235	21676	39559
46	5015	2589	2426				
47	4897	2494	2403				
48	4967	2492	2475				
49	4735	2343	2392				

*   45 – 64 for males; 45 – 59 for females.
**   65 and over for males; 60 and over for females.

Table P5

Population at Census Day 2001: Resident population by single year of age and sex

Age	All Persons	Males	Females	Age	All Persons	Males	Females
All ages	274878	134798	140080	50-54	15623	7844	7779
				50	3181	1625	1556
0-4	20391	10484	9907	51	3195	1593	1602
0	3745	1878	1867	52	3083	1569	1514
1	3872	2055	1817	53	3013	1470	1543
2	4189	2138	2051	54	3151	1587	1564
3	4178	2120	2058				
4	4407	2293	2114	55-59	13656	6704	6952
				55	2804	1415	1389
5-9	20798	10543	10255	56	2778	1341	1437
5	4135	2128	2007	57	2891	1444	1447
6	4095	2069	2026	58	2722	1294	1428
7	4053	2043	2010	59	2461	1210	1251
8	4244	2140	2104				
9	4271	2163	2108	60-64	11738	5691	6047
				60	2423	1170	1253
10-14	23231	11905	11326	61	2323	1147	1176
10	4540	2297	2243	62	2363	1135	1228
11	4513	2309	2204	63	2325	1156	1169
12	4570	2343	2227	64	2304	1083	1221
13	4760	2433	2327				
14	4848	2523	2325	65-69	9661	4561	5100
				65	2058	983	1075
15-19	22558	11585	10973	66	1962	948	1014
15	4755	2516	2239	67	1885	870	1015
16	4737	2468	2269	68	1907	892	1015
17	4648	2378	2270	69	1849	868	981
18	4412	2221	2191				
19	4006	2002	2004	70-74	8361	3684	4677
				70	1844	842	1002
20-24	18639	9250	9389	71	1716	787	929
20	3950	1931	2019	72	1700	720	980
21	3884	1963	1921	73	1550	650	900
22	3620	1772	1848	74	1551	685	866
23	3552	1713	1839				
24	3633	1871	1762	75-79	6573	2640	3933
				75	1536	638	898
25-29	19402	9451	9951	76	1360	573	787
25	3599	1754	1845	77	1314	528	786
26	3606	1738	1868	78	1203	457	746
27	3805	1851	1954	79	1160	444	716
28	4134	2028	2106				
29	4258	2080	2178	80-84	4174	1560	2614
				80	1060	411	649
30-34	21037	10346	10691	81	991	377	614
30	4180	2044	2136	82	835	312	523
31	4114	2008	2106	83	692	252	440
32	4207	2076	2131	84	596	208	388
33	4317	2129	2188				
34	4219	2089	2130	85-89	2158	625	1533
				85	519	169	350
35-39	21073	10340	10733	86	490	166	324
35	4382	2143	2239	87	474	123	351
36	4426	2154	2272	88	381	95	286
37	4162	2103	2059	89	294	72	222
38	4039	1956	2083				
39	4064	1984	2080	90 and over	876	205	671
40-44	18543	9153	9390	Under 16	69175	35448	33727
40	3995	2022	1973				
41	3794	1887	1907	Under 18	78560	40294	38266
42	3672	1793	1879				
43	3544	1716	1828	16-44	116497	57609	58888
44	3538	1735	1803				
				45-59/64*	51356	28466	22890
45-49	16386	8227	8159				
45	3435	1700	1735	60/65** and over	37850	13275	24575
46	3386	1761	1625				
47	3317	1667	1650				
48	3195	1617	1578				
49	3053	1482	1571				

* 45 – 64 for males; 45 – 59 for females.
** 65 and over for males; 60 and over for females.

Table P5

Population at Census Day 2001: Resident population by single year of age and sex

Age	All Persons	Males	Females
All ages	366896	182727	184169
0-4	27254	13903	13351
0	5065	2629	2436
1	5476	2703	2773
2	5527	2775	2752
3	5605	2952	2653
4	5581	2844	2737
5-9	28633	14730	13903
5	5697	3001	2696
6	5631	2926	2705
7	5708	2911	2797
8	5678	2902	2776
9	5919	2990	2929
10-14	31686	16288	15398
10	6178	3179	2999
11	6255	3192	3063
12	6325	3287	3038
13	6345	3261	3084
14	6583	3369	3214
15-19	30222	15443	14779
15	6555	3301	3254
16	6645	3387	3258
17	6592	3290	3302
18	6124	3133	2991
19	4306	2332	1974
20-24	23463	12370	11093
20	4458	2428	2030
21	4584	2463	2121
22	4801	2516	2285
23	4783	2493	2290
24	4837	2470	2367
25-29	25649	12854	12795
25	4844	2509	2335
26	4752	2404	2348
27	5257	2699	2558
28	5318	2598	2720
29	5478	2644	2834
30-34	26803	13538	13265
30	5567	2879	2688
31	5349	2685	2664
32	5324	2594	2730
33	5424	2764	2660
34	5139	2616	2523
35-39	26954	13616	13338
35	5418	2722	2696
36	5537	2834	2703
37	5512	2732	2780
38	5379	2783	2596
39	5108	2545	2563
40-44	25218	12604	12614
40	5351	2651	2700
41	5173	2542	2631
42	4831	2455	2376
43	5016	2469	2547
44	4847	2487	2360
45-49	22496	11578	10918
45	4763	2461	2302
46	4541	2334	2207
47	4505	2342	2163
48	4445	2313	2132
49	4242	2128	2114

Age	All Persons	Males	Females
50-54	20945	10459	10486
50	4225	2120	2105
51	4213	2104	2109
52	4278	2098	2180
53	4094	2057	2037
54	4135	2080	2055
55-59	17988	8977	9011
55	3795	1914	1881
56	3782	1860	1922
57	3673	1871	1802
58	3501	1740	1761
59	3237	1592	1645
60-64	14999	7412	7587
60	3067	1512	1555
61	3159	1593	1566
62	3018	1471	1547
63	2820	1403	1417
64	2935	1433	1502
65-69	13277	6364	6913
65	2860	1387	1473
66	2650	1311	1339
67	2702	1292	1410
68	2550	1172	1378
69	2515	1202	1313
70-74	11480	5073	6407
70	2387	1050	1337
71	2419	1110	1309
72	2252	1002	1250
73	2215	933	1282
74	2207	978	1229
75-79	9354	3903	5451
75	2059	901	1158
76	1969	831	1138
77	1894	799	1095
78	1808	718	1090
79	1624	654	970
80-84	6024	2270	3754
80	1506	590	916
81	1413	528	885
82	1205	476	729
83	975	362	613
84	925	314	611
85-89	3177	1009	2168
85	838	279	559
86	763	239	524
87	618	204	414
88	537	171	366
89	421	116	305
90 and over	1274	336	938
Under 16	94128	48222	45906
Under 18	107365	54899	52466
16-44	151754	77124	74630
45-59/64*	68841	38426	30415
60/65** and over	52173	18955	33218

*   45 – 64 for males; 45 – 59 for females.
**   65 and over for males; 60 and over for females.

Table P6

Population at Census Day 2001: Resident population by single year of age and sex

Age	All Persons	Males	Females	Age	All Persons	Males	Females
All ages	58789194	28581233	30207961	50-54	4040437	2003224	2037213
				50	739798	366654	373144
0-4	3486469	1786036	1700433	51	765279	378580	386699
0	660080	337377	322703	52	789112	391556	397556
1	680725	349379	331346	53	852869	422732	430137
2	699913	358581	341332	54	893379	443702	449677
3	712460	364693	347767				
4	733291	376006	357285	55-59	3338861	1651417	1687444
				55	689196	341514	347682
5-9	3738160	1914865	1823295	56	710966	351977	358989
5	721433	369897	351536	57	689867	342107	347760
6	726866	372841	354025	58	659506	325880	333626
7	747704	382836	364868	59	589326	289939	299387
8	757129	387616	369513				
9	785028	401675	383353	60-64	2879948	1409676	1470272
				60	559590	274340	285250
10-14	3880609	1987690	1892919	61	591509	290156	301353
10	791067	405364	385703	62	586244	286718	299526
11	774646	396875	377771	63	579076	283752	295324
12	770701	394666	376035	64	563529	274710	288819
13	783855	401690	382165				
14	760340	389095	371245	65-69	2596843	1241382	1355461
				65	547286	265074	282212
15-19	3663899	1870622	1793277	66	530226	255997	274229
15	763913	392047	371866	67	507487	242799	264688
16	758448	389019	369429	68	505819	239563	266256
17	726698	372622	354076	69	506025	237949	268076
18	712268	363037	349231				
19	702572	353897	348675	70-74	2339231	1059151	1280080
				70	503581	232941	270640
20-24	3546151	1765417	1780734	71	486241	222094	264147
20	745538	374537	371001	72	466129	210925	255204
21	739260	370320	368940	73	443669	198815	244854
22	706745	352055	354690	74	439611	194376	245235
23	673770	333081	340689				
24	680838	335424	345414	75-79	1966929	817711	1149218
				75	426751	185463	241288
25-29	3867115	1895543	1971572	76	405387	172271	233116
25	700076	344003	356073	77	389535	161798	227737
26	730325	357838	372487	78	372571	150821	221750
27	760105	372089	388016	79	372685	147358	225327
28	814122	399467	414655				
29	862487	422146	440341	80-84	1313547	482697	830850
				80	368167	141490	226677
30-34	4493585	2199874	2293711	81	337780	127790	209990
30	878633	429100	449533	82	221508	80383	141125
31	869849	426098	443751	83	188740	66027	122713
32	902531	441077	461454	84	197352	67007	130345
33	908253	444492	463761				
34	934319	459107	475212	85-89	752787	226833	525954
				85	184524	59873	124651
35-39	4625810	2277799	2348011	86	177304	54981	122323
35	930987	457028	473959	87	153053	45407	107646
36	942077	463452	478625	88	130373	37269	93104
37	933667	459412	474255	89	107533	29303	78230
38	920581	453903	466678				
39	898498	444004	454494	90 and over	371269	83202	288067
40-44	4151580	2056630	2094950				
40	874182	432141	442041				
41	840271	416459	423812				
42	828071	410266	417805				
43	818896	406161	412735				
44	790160	391603	398557				
45-49	3735964	1851464	1884500				
45	762294	378146	384148				
46	744666	368996	375670				
47	753123	373083	380040				
48	741433	367448	373985				
49	734448	363791	370657				

Table P7

Population at Census Day 2001: Resident population by five year age bands

Age	United Kingdom	Northern Ireland	England	Scotland	Wales
All Ages	58789194	1685267	49138831	5062011	2903085
0-4	3486469	115238	2926460	276874	167897
5-9	3738160	123050	3122646	307138	185326
10-14	3880609	132664	3229098	322870	195977
15-19	3663899	129201	3032714	317273	184711
20-24	3546151	109385	2952885	314387	169494
25-29	3867115	114704	3268760	317303	166348
30-34	4493585	127517	3785676	382094	198298
35-39	4625810	129639	3881043	402954	212174
40-44	4151580	117335	3460849	377910	195486
45-49	3735964	102464	3111538	337469	184493
50-54	4040437	98426	3382567	351107	208337
55-59	3338861	88732	2785286	287999	176844
60-64	2879948	73587	2391708	261733	152920
65-69	2596843	65341	2153925	239116	138461
70-74	2339231	57852	1948731	206917	125731
75-79	1966929	46542	1645033	165523	109831
80-84	1313547	30289	1105896	104989	72373
85-89	752787	16116	638384	59241	39046
90 and over	371269	7185	315632	29114	19338

CENSUS

Table P7

Population at Census Day 2001: Male population by five year age bands

Age	United Kingdom	Northern Ireland	England	Scotland	Wales
All Ages	28581233	821449	23923390	2432494	1403900
0-4	1786036	59213	1498354	142360	86109
5-9	1914865	63147	1599932	157030	94756
10-14	1987690	68014	1653107	165583	100986
15-19	1870622	65598	1550903	160935	93186
20-24	1765417	54913	1469004	157116	84384
25-29	1895543	56628	1603559	154112	81244
30-34	2199874	62487	1857168	184674	95545
35-39	2277799	63430	1915937	194618	103814
40-44	2056630	57432	1719412	184176	95610
45-49	1851464	51686	1541999	166925	90854
50-54	2003224	48484	1677360	174118	103262
55-59	1651417	43585	1379477	140835	87520
60-64	1409676	35401	1174449	124651	75175
65-69	1241382	30406	1034649	110009	66318
70-74	1059151	25069	886793	90053	57236
75-79	817711	18562	687287	66057	45805
80-84	482697	11090	408958	36355	26294
85-89	226833	4707	193860	16661	11605
90 and over	83202	1597	71182	6226	4197

Table P7

Population at Census Day 2001: Female population by five year age bands

Age	United Kingdom	Northern Ireland	England	Scotland	Wales
All Ages	30207961	863818	25215441	2629517	1499185
0-4	1700433	56025	1428106	134514	81788
5-9	1823295	59903	1522714	150108	90570
10-14	1892919	64650	1575991	157287	94991
15-19	1793277	63603	1481811	156338	91525
20-24	1780734	54472	1483881	157271	85110
25-29	1971572	58076	1665201	163191	85104
30-34	2293711	65030	1928508	197420	102753
35-39	2348011	66209	1965106	208336	108360
40-44	2094950	59903	1741437	193734	99876
45-49	1884500	50778	1569539	170544	93639
50-54	2037213	49942	1705207	176989	105075
55-59	1687444	45147	1405809	147164	89324
60-64	1470272	38186	1217259	137082	77745
65-69	1355461	34935	1119276	129107	72143
70-74	1280080	32783	1061938	116864	68495
75-79	1149218	27980	957746	99466	64026
80-84	830850	19199	696938	68634	46079
85-89	525954	11409	444524	42580	27441
90 and over	288067	5588	244450	22888	15141

CENSUS

Mid-Year Population Estimates

Table M1

Mid-Year Population at 30 June 2001: Resident population by single year of age and sex

Age	All Persons	Males	Females	Age	All Persons	Males	Females
All Ages	1689319	824429	864890	50-54	98237	48423	49814
				50	19444	9746	9698
0-4	114749	59075	55674	51	19642	9712	9930
0	21513	11127	10386	52	19545	9641	9904
1	22298	11511	10787	53	19619	9581	10038
2	23118	11824	11294	54	19987	9743	10244
3	23565	12172	11393				
4	24255	12441	11814	55-59	89353	43862	45491
				55	18436	9142	9294
5-9	122853	63019	59834	56	18153	8894	9259
5	23963	12430	11533	57	18358	9030	9328
6	24065	12398	11667	58	18074	8820	9254
7	24330	12369	11961	59	16332	7976	8356
8	24833	12623	12210				
9	25662	13199	12463	60-64	73719	35474	38245
				60	14977	7286	7691
10-14	132442	67891	64551	61	14794	7145	7649
10	26119	13402	12717	62	14947	7156	7791
11	26009	13291	12718	63	14468	6982	7486
12	26326	13527	12799	64	14533	6905	7628
13	26881	13738	13143				
14	27107	13933	13174	65-69	65503	30487	35016
				65	13970	6596	7374
15-19	129870	66037	63833	66	13277	6299	6978
15	27106	13904	13202	67	12944	6031	6913
16	27154	13857	13297	68	12779	5802	6977
17	26410	13380	13030	69	12533	5759	6774
18	25548	13065	12483				
19	23652	11831	11821	70-74	57852	25090	32762
				70	12435	5508	6927
20-24	110392	55557	54835	71	12019	5280	6739
20	22876	11661	11215	72	11467	4983	6484
21	22714	11657	11057	73	10977	4652	6325
22	22036	11026	11010	74	10954	4667	6287
23	21380	10574	10806				
24	21386	10639	10747	75-79	46650	18650	28000
				75	10508	4343	6165
25-29	114864	56958	57906	76	9825	4067	5758
25	21689	10848	10841	77	9267	3741	5526
26	21717	10750	10967	78	8721	3352	5369
27	22918	11387	11531	79	8329	3147	5182
28	24028	11872	12156				
29	24512	12101	12411	80-84	30537	11181	19356
				80	7891	3018	4873
30-34	127949	62965	64984	81	7311	2751	4560
30	25324	12508	12816	82	5977	2208	3769
31	25163	12406	12757	83	4906	1703	3203
32	25554	12507	13047	84	4452	1501	2951
33	25856	12733	13123				
34	26052	12811	13241	85-89	16156	4747	11409
				85	4064	1278	2786
35-39	130230	63911	66319	86	3755	1127	2628
35	26170	12934	13236	87	3273	958	2315
36	26846	13183	13663	88	2807	801	2006
37	26374	12936	13438	89	2257	583	1674
38	25763	12691	13072				
39	25077	12167	12910	90 and over	7268	1617	5651
40-44	117801	57642	60159	Under 16	397150	203889	193261
40	24849	12181	12668				
41	24185	11841	12344	Under 18	450714	231126	219588
42	23210	11326	11884				
43	23224	11351	11873	16-44	704000	349166	354834
44	22333	10943	11390				
				45-59/64*	325958	179602	146356
45-49	102894	51843	51051				
45	21793	10892	10901	60/65** and over	262211	91772	170439
46	20783	10560	10223				
47	20512	10433	10079				
48	20312	10201	10111				
49	19494	9757	9737				

* 45 – 64 for males; 45 – 59 for females.

** 65 and over for males; 60 and over for females.

MID-YEAR ESTIMATES

Table M2

Mid-Year Population at 30 June 2001: Resident population by single year of age and sex

Age	All Persons	Males	Females	Age	All Persons	Males	Females
All Ages	48761	24590	24171	50-54	2934	1482	1452
				50	569	290	279
0-4	3603	1847	1756	51	584	288	296
0	711	374	337	52	582	306	276
1	720	381	339	53	580	290	290
2	738	374	364	54	619	308	311
3	700	348	352				
4	734	370	364	55-59	2712	1325	1387
				55	547	266	281
5-9	3676	1878	1798	56	528	251	277
5	752	394	358	57	548	271	277
6	719	361	358	58	565	288	277
7	755	388	367	59	524	249	275
8	736	385	351				
9	714	350	364	60-64	2052	994	1058
				60	453	201	252
10-14	3630	1867	1763	61	410	187	223
10	733	383	350	62	408	197	211
11	721	358	363	63	396	209	187
12	685	349	336	64	385	200	185
13	751	387	364				
14	740	390	350	65-69	1619	783	836
				65	347	178	169
15-19	3401	1764	1637	66	348	165	183
15	719	371	348	67	307	147	160
16	702	360	342	68	306	142	164
17	667	343	324	69	311	151	160
18	691	352	339				
19	622	338	284	70-74	1312	610	702
				70	310	155	155
20-24	3144	1684	1460	71	277	125	152
20	615	347	268	72	246	116	130
21	664	324	340	73	238	105	133
22	635	350	285	74	241	109	132
23	606	328	278				
24	624	335	289	75-79	1003	415	588
				75	212	89	123
25-29	3769	2010	1759	76	226	100	126
25	668	348	320	77	187	82	105
26	709	377	332	78	198	79	119
27	772	425	347	79	180	65	115
28	761	401	360				
29	859	459	400	80-84	677	250	427
				80	166	65	101
30-34	4316	2246	2070	81	161	53	108
30	860	449	411	82	148	57	91
31	870	451	419	83	117	45	72
32	877	462	415	84	85	30	55
33	859	443	416				
34	850	441	409	85-89	358	96	262
				85	89	25	64
35-39	4146	2144	2002	86	89	23	66
35	855	454	401	87	70	17	53
36	879	446	433	88	57	18	39
37	867	446	421	89	53	13	40
38	834	434	400				
39	711	364	347	90 and over	181	51	130
40-44	3270	1656	1614	Under 16	11628	5963	5665
40	689	348	341				
41	666	339	327	Under 18	12997	6666	6331
42	642	329	313				
43	641	316	325	16-44	21327	11133	10194
44	632	324	308				
				45-59/64*	9598	5289	4309
45-49	2958	1488	1470				
45	620	308	312	60/65** and over	6208	2205	4003
46	628	329	299				
47	560	288	272				
48	574	279	295	* 45 – 64 for males; 45 – 59 for females.			
49	576	284	292	** 65 and over for males; 60 and over for females.			

MID-YEAR ESTIMATES

Table M2

Mid-Year Population at 30 June 2001: Resident population by single year of age and sex

Age	All Persons	Males	Females	Age	All Persons	Males	Females
All Ages	73435	35836	37599	50-54	5167	2527	2640
0-4	4614	2382	2232	50	944	475	469
0	810	411	399	51	1019	479	540
1	916	463	453	52	1027	497	530
2	964	499	465	53	1096	541	555
3	966	506	460	54	1081	535	546
4	958	503	455	55-59	4777	2406	2371
5-9	4804	2460	2344	55	1010	508	502
5	947	488	459	56	984	497	487
6	946	478	468	57	954	485	469
7	936	488	448	58	960	473	487
8	978	491	487	59	869	443	426
9	997	515	482	60-64	3481	1681	1800
10-14	5120	2659	2461	60	719	351	368
10	1009	517	492	61	683	322	361
11	1008	526	482	62	721	340	381
12	1041	541	500	63	689	330	359
13	1051	548	503	64	669	338	331
14	1011	527	484	65-69	2916	1389	1527
15-19	4896	2491	2405	65	615	306	309
15	1030	508	522	66	611	309	302
16	1044	530	514	67	571	280	291
17	1007	514	493	68	573	252	321
18	998	510	488	69	546	242	304
19	817	429	388	70-74	2623	1137	1486
20-24	4080	2019	2061	70	550	237	313
20	853	428	425	71	534	222	312
21	816	432	384	72	515	226	289
22	792	382	410	73	520	239	281
23	832	408	424	74	504	213	291
24	787	369	418	75-79	2103	879	1224
25-29	4583	2308	2275	75	483	196	287
25	862	439	423	76	435	185	250
26	824	419	405	77	401	184	217
27	931	474	457	78	390	163	227
28	959	458	501	79	394	151	243
29	1007	518	489	80-84	1548	593	955
30-34	5571	2728	2843	80	390	150	240
30	1057	500	557	81	375	135	240
31	1028	497	531	82	285	109	176
32	1122	576	546	83	265	113	152
33	1197	594	603	84	233	86	147
34	1167	561	606	85-89	783	238	545
35-39	5764	2786	2978	85	187	61	126
35	1145	579	566	86	192	57	135
36	1198	591	607	87	162	54	108
37	1124	533	591	88	141	41	100
38	1159	570	589	89	101	25	76
39	1138	513	625	90 and over	369	90	279
40-44	5436	2677	2759	Under 16	15568	8009	7559
40	1148	565	583	Under 18	17619	9053	8566
41	1129	554	575	16-44	29300	14501	14799
42	1056	514	542	45-59/64*	16425	9000	7425
43	1095	531	564	60/65** and over	12142	4326	7816
44	1008	513	495				
45-49	4800	2386	2414				
45	980	503	477				
46	955	471	484				
47	947	468	479				
48	965	484	481				
49	953	460	493				

*   45 – 64 for males; 45 – 59 for females.
** 65 and over for males; 60 and over for females.

MID-YEAR ESTIMATES

57

Table M2

Mid-Year Population at 30 June 2001: Resident population by single year of age and sex

Age	All Persons	Males	Females	Age	All Persons	Males	Females
All Ages	54462	27041	27421	50-54	3219	1597	1622
				50	618	312	306
0-4	3973	1995	1978	51	647	323	324
0	722	365	357	52	652	330	322
1	843	390	453	53	650	313	337
2	816	414	402	54	652	319	333
3	810	423	387				
4	782	403	379	55-59	2834	1423	1411
				55	603	306	297
5-9	4136	2123	2013	56	582	289	293
5	804	419	385	57	568	275	293
6	822	422	400	58	552	283	269
7	816	404	412	59	529	270	259
8	813	408	405				
9	881	470	411	60-64	2341	1148	1193
				60	480	241	239
10-14	4546	2346	2200	61	481	235	246
10	882	440	442	62	479	227	252
11	888	458	430	63	452	230	222
12	909	480	429	64	449	215	234
13	925	484	441				
14	942	484	458	65-69	1987	944	1043
				65	433	206	227
15-19	4420	2254	2166	66	407	196	211
15	930	474	456	67	413	194	219
16	1016	511	505	68	371	166	205
17	918	462	456	69	363	182	181
18	869	450	419				
19	687	357	330	70-74	1757	742	1015
				70	367	156	211
20-24	3478	1840	1638	71	385	164	221
20	673	372	301	72	353	151	202
21	674	370	304	73	355	144	211
22	692	359	333	74	297	127	170
23	717	357	360				
24	722	382	340	75-79	1399	564	835
				75	328	135	193
25-29	3771	1844	1927	76	295	115	180
25	702	356	346	77	280	112	168
26	668	340	328	78	261	110	151
27	768	398	370	79	235	92	143
28	782	379	403				
29	851	371	480	80-84	887	323	564
				80	226	88	138
30-34	3943	1995	1948	81	204	72	132
30	798	383	415	82	197	69	128
31	782	418	364	83	138	58	80
32	793	403	390	84	122	36	86
33	789	413	376				
34	781	378	403	85-89	444	132	312
				85	107	33	74
35-39	4062	2059	2003	86	106	37	69
35	776	403	373	87	93	27	66
36	843	427	416	88	76	21	55
37	844	432	412	89	62	14	48
38	805	404	401				
39	794	393	401	90 and over	185	49	136
40-44	3792	1957	1835	Under 16	13585	6938	6647
40	790	404	386				
41	792	393	399	Under 18	15519	7911	7608
42	740	375	365				
43	767	408	359	16-44	22536	11475	11061
44	703	377	326				
				45-59/64*	10489	5874	4615
45-49	3288	1706	1582				
45	695	363	332	60/65** and over	7852	2754	5098
46	657	337	320				
47	639	317	322				
48	689	378	311				
49	608	311	297				

*   45 – 64 for males; 45 – 59 for females.
** 65 and over for males; 60 and over for females.

MID-YEAR ESTIMATES

Table M2

Mid-Year Population at 30 June 2001: Resident population by single year of age and sex

Age	All Persons	Males	Females	Age	All Persons	Males	Females
All Ages	58801	28668	30133	50-54	3748	1852	1896
				50	734	378	356
0-4	3767	1905	1862	51	777	398	379
0	747	397	350	52	744	363	381
1	738	379	359	53	717	335	382
2	742	374	368	54	776	378	398
3	756	378	378				
4	784	377	407	55-59	3495	1695	1800
				55	752	363	389
5-9	3958	2040	1918	56	690	344	346
5	754	365	389	57	716	363	353
6	780	395	385	58	694	319	375
7	795	411	384	59	643	306	337
8	800	414	386				
9	829	455	374	60-64	2877	1390	1487
				60	557	268	289
10-14	4290	2210	2080	61	596	284	312
10	788	413	375	62	600	298	302
11	812	417	395	63	573	278	295
12	851	446	405	64	551	262	289
13	923	460	463				
14	916	474	442	65-69	2509	1193	1316
				65	539	261	278
15-19	4166	2139	2027	66	527	243	284
15	881	465	416	67	503	245	258
16	883	468	415	68	493	230	263
17	875	438	437	69	447	214	233
18	865	437	428				
19	662	331	331	70-74	2172	936	1236
				70	455	184	271
20-24	3388	1712	1676	71	450	193	257
20	691	380	311	72	455	209	246
21	663	346	317	73	386	170	216
22	700	342	358	74	426	180	246
23	666	325	341				
24	668	319	349	75-79	1758	720	1038
				75	405	169	236
25-29	3756	1867	1889	76	365	159	206
25	679	329	350	77	343	145	198
26	672	315	357	78	346	127	219
27	762	392	370	79	299	120	179
28	809	415	394				
29	834	416	418	80-84	1149	428	721
				80	300	123	177
30-34	4638	2309	2329	81	238	90	148
30	917	462	455	82	232	74	158
31	896	443	453	83	192	69	123
32	949	474	475	84	187	72	115
33	938	458	480				
34	938	472	466	85-89	628	186	442
				85	149	49	100
35-39	4375	2120	2255	86	139	43	96
35	893	442	451	87	134	42	92
36	925	445	480	88	110	35	75
37	876	431	445	89	96	17	79
38	880	421	459				
39	801	381	420	90 and over	289	61	228
40-44	3957	1972	1985	Under 16	12896	6620	6276
40	809	402	407				
41	806	396	410	Under 18	14654	7526	7128
42	791	412	379				
43	790	391	399	16-44	23399	11654	11745
44	761	371	390				
				45-59/64*	12514	6870	5644
45-49	3881	1933	1948				
45	807	416	391	60/65** and over	9992	3524	6468
46	797	393	404				
47	756	379	377				
48	783	377	406	* 45 – 64 for males; 45 – 59 for females.			
49	738	368	370	** 65 and over for males; 60 and over for females.			

MID-YEAR ESTIMATES

59

Table M2

Mid-Year Population at 30 June 2001: Resident population by single year of age and sex

Age	All Persons	Males	Females	Age	All Persons	Males	Females
All Ages	27007	13349	13658	50-54	1524	791	733
				50	298	165	133
0-4	1907	973	934	51	317	161	156
0	345	167	178	52	305	152	153
1	375	202	173	53	295	148	147
2	393	211	182	54	309	165	144
3	390	182	208				
4	404	211	193	55-59	1499	722	777
				55	290	143	147
5-9	1899	991	908	56	289	141	148
5	371	197	174	57	315	157	158
6	392	210	182	58	324	158	166
7	369	183	186	59	281	123	158
8	387	204	183				
9	380	197	183	60-64	1221	596	625
				60	257	117	140
10-14	2150	1084	1066	61	262	134	128
10	431	201	230	62	251	132	119
11	443	225	218	63	229	112	117
12	407	213	194	64	222	101	121
13	421	219	202				
14	448	226	222	65-69	1039	482	557
				65	200	85	115
15-19	1999	1015	984	66	221	105	116
15	418	227	191	67	220	103	117
16	445	232	213	68	207	98	109
17	419	210	209	69	191	91	100
18	393	182	211				
19	324	164	160	70-74	963	420	543
				70	207	93	114
20-24	1570	817	753	71	201	93	108
20	321	179	142	72	188	76	112
21	306	161	145	73	183	77	106
22	294	141	153	74	184	81	103
23	313	144	169				
24	336	192	144	75-79	778	328	450
				75	160	66	94
25-29	1864	943	921	76	158	69	89
25	328	157	171	77	166	75	91
26	325	159	166	78	155	61	94
27	352	182	170	79	139	57	82
28	396	193	203				
29	463	252	211	80-84	549	203	346
				80	137	57	80
30-34	2153	1104	1049	81	135	54	81
30	459	257	202	82	110	38	72
31	427	204	223	83	89	26	63
32	438	217	221	84	78	28	50
33	435	220	215				
34	394	206	188	85-89	222	69	153
				85	59	16	43
35-39	2088	1034	1054	86	48	15	33
35	421	203	218	87	40	12	28
36	444	234	210	88	45	18	27
37	417	216	201	89	30	8	22
38	376	183	193				
39	430	198	232	90 and over	96	21	75
40-44	1843	925	918	Under 16	6374	3275	3099
40	401	201	200				
41	380	191	189	Under 18	7238	3717	3521
42	356	194	162				
43	329	164	165	16-44	11099	5611	5488
44	377	175	202				
				45-59/64*	5262	2940	2322
45-49	1643	831	812				
45	388	198	190	60/65** and over	4272	1523	2749
46	329	166	163				
47	324	163	161				
48	300	159	141				
49	302	145	157				

*   45 – 64 for males; 45 – 59 for females.
**   65 and over for males; 60 and over for females.

MID-YEAR ESTIMATES

Table M2

Mid-Year Population at 30 June 2001: Resident population by single year of age and sex

Age	All Persons	Males	Females	Age	All Persons	Males	Females
All Ages	41549	20803	20746	50-54	2357	1133	1224
				50	470	226	244
0-4	2956	1581	1375	51	474	234	240
0	568	305	263	52	460	227	233
1	565	308	257	53	486	226	260
2	595	315	280	54	467	220	247
3	608	325	283				
4	620	328	292	55-59	2190	1114	1076
				55	437	222	215
5-9	3010	1593	1417	56	464	248	216
5	597	306	291	57	426	226	200
6	632	349	283	58	448	225	223
7	596	321	275	59	415	193	222
8	587	317	270				
9	598	300	298	60-64	1762	830	932
				60	385	174	211
10-14	3160	1655	1505	61	351	167	184
10	617	350	267	62	332	159	173
11	610	317	293	63	339	157	182
12	641	344	297	64	355	173	182
13	635	310	325				
14	657	334	323	65-69	1574	726	848
				65	337	162	175
15-19	3031	1569	1462	66	302	139	163
15	648	331	317	67	319	144	175
16	647	323	324	68	304	137	167
17	606	325	281	69	312	144	168
18	599	324	275				
19	531	266	265	70-74	1303	602	701
				70	299	146	153
20-24	2433	1227	1206	71	266	121	145
20	492	266	226	72	261	120	141
21	510	246	264	73	234	114	120
22	463	236	227	74	243	101	142
23	470	244	226				
24	498	235	263	75-79	1056	434	622
				75	248	111	137
25-29	2871	1449	1422	76	227	99	128
25	525	278	247	77	209	80	129
26	513	262	251	78	189	71	118
27	567	276	291	79	183	73	110
28	599	300	299				
29	667	333	334	80-84	720	263	457
				80	173	64	109
30-34	3462	1804	1658	81	170	61	109
30	676	348	328	82	152	54	98
31	717	369	348	83	126	45	81
32	664	343	321	84	99	39	60
33	678	350	328				
34	727	394	333	85-89	395	138	257
				85	107	35	72
35-39	3451	1762	1689	86	98	34	64
35	692	350	342	87	70	28	42
36	697	360	337	88	73	29	44
37	698	365	333	89	47	12	35
38	679	357	322				
39	685	330	355	90 and over	163	34	129
40-44	3015	1482	1533	Under 16	9774	5160	4614
40	608	293	315				
41	605	287	318	Under 18	11027	5808	5219
42	628	301	327				
43	594	298	296	16-44	17615	8962	8653
44	580	303	277				
45-49	2640	1407	1233	45-59/64*	8017	4484	3533
45	604	320	284				
46	549	299	250	60/65** and over	6143	2197	3946
47	514	271	243				
48	512	286	226				
49	461	231	230				

*   45 – 64 for males; 45 – 59 for females.
** 65 and over for males; 60 and over for females.

Table M2

Mid-Year Population at 30 June 2001: Resident population by single year of age and sex

Age	All Persons	Males	Females	Age	All Persons	Males	Females
All Ages	277170	129804	147366	50-54	14173	6847	7326
				50	2832	1395	1437
0-4	16499	8439	8060	51	2803	1333	1470
0	3229	1625	1604	52	2720	1323	1397
1	3136	1651	1485	53	2855	1394	1461
2	3252	1689	1563	54	2963	1402	1561
3	3328	1707	1621				
4	3554	1767	1787	55-59	13701	6546	7155
				55	2749	1340	1409
5-9	18615	9444	9171	56	2709	1303	1406
5	3415	1746	1669	57	2784	1315	1469
6	3535	1768	1767	58	2874	1357	1517
7	3724	1842	1882	59	2585	1231	1354
8	3902	1970	1932				
9	4039	2118	1921	60-64	12100	5673	6427
				60	2295	1111	1184
10-14	20525	10444	10081	61	2386	1128	1258
10	3985	2040	1945	62	2449	1129	1320
11	3921	1962	1959	63	2475	1151	1324
12	4124	2109	2015	64	2495	1154	1341
13	4251	2137	2114				
14	4244	2196	2048	65-69	11690	5141	6549
				65	2444	1069	1375
15-19	22340	10971	11369	66	2318	1024	1294
15	4307	2190	2117	67	2308	1034	1274
16	4288	2197	2091	68	2297	989	1308
17	4053	2074	1979	69	2323	1025	1298
18	4198	2128	2070				
19	5494	2382	3112	70-74	11001	4451	6550
				70	2366	957	1409
20-24	23526	11118	12408	71	2318	941	1377
20	5379	2416	2963	72	2130	873	1257
21	5099	2397	2702	73	2094	848	1246
22	4669	2229	2440	74	2093	832	1261
23	4222	2033	2189				
24	4157	2043	2114	75-79	8982	3339	5643
				75	2019	797	1222
25-29	20226	9662	10564	76	1929	756	1173
25	4209	2018	2191	77	1769	625	1144
26	4083	1959	2124	78	1650	596	1054
27	4051	1887	2164	79	1615	565	1050
28	4106	1969	2137				
29	3777	1829	1948	80-84	5891	1986	3905
				80	1572	560	1012
30-34	19564	9163	10401	81	1460	525	935
30	3941	1859	2082	82	1125	385	740
31	3897	1862	2035	83	900	268	632
32	3850	1778	2072	84	834	248	586
33	3848	1818	2030				
34	4028	1846	2182	85-89	3276	906	2370
				85	785	229	556
35-39	19857	9311	10546	86	791	236	555
35	3980	1877	2103	87	681	192	489
36	4039	1921	2118	88	566	137	429
37	4062	1921	2141	89	453	112	341
38	3902	1809	2093				
39	3874	1783	2091	90 and over	1534	300	1234
40-44	18414	8554	9860	Under 16	59946	30517	29429
40	3871	1811	2060				
41	3735	1756	1979	Under 18	68287	34788	33499
42	3641	1650	1991				
43	3647	1721	1926	16-44	119620	56589	63031
44	3520	1616	1904				
				45-59/64*	48803	26575	22228
45-49	15256	7509	7747				
45	3263	1561	1702	60/65** and over	48801	16123	32678
46	3071	1509	1562				
47	3053	1506	1547				
48	3024	1482	1542	* 45 – 64 for males; 45 – 59 for females.			
49	2845	1451	1394	** 65 and over for males; 60 and over for females.			

Carrickfergus Local Government District

Table M2

Mid-Year Population at 30 June 2001: Resident population by single year of age and sex

Age	All Persons	Males	Females	Age	All Persons	Males	Females
All Ages	37730	18301	19429	50-54	2201	1080	1121
				50	462	242	220
0-4	2426	1279	1147	51	450	233	217
0	473	267	206	52	391	183	208
1	472	244	228	53	438	207	231
2	472	241	231	54	460	215	245
3	503	261	242				
4	506	266	240	55-59	2101	1024	1077
				55	417	207	210
5-9	2667	1368	1299	56	425	215	210
5	518	262	256	57	440	195	245
6	530	280	250	58	430	222	208
7	539	278	261	59	389	185	204
8	530	258	272				
9	550	290	260	60-64	1683	829	854
				60	346	187	159
10-14	2776	1379	1397	61	342	169	173
10	525	247	278	62	324	152	172
11	575	290	285	63	339	164	175
12	556	274	282	64	332	157	175
13	552	280	272				
14	568	288	280	65-69	1526	701	825
				65	329	157	172
15-19	2632	1367	1265	66	303	142	161
15	603	310	293	67	318	139	179
16	555	302	253	68	299	139	160
17	505	265	240	69	277	124	153
18	507	272	235				
19	462	218	244	70-74	1291	564	727
				70	300	126	174
20-24	2214	1062	1152	71	265	120	145
20	488	255	233	72	245	109	136
21	430	221	209	73	238	101	137
22	405	187	218	74	243	108	135
23	454	205	249				
24	437	194	243	75-79	1060	414	646
				75	220	85	135
25-29	2395	1162	1233	76	212	93	119
25	395	175	220	77	225	95	130
26	444	216	228	78	210	76	134
27	471	233	238	79	193	65	128
28	550	282	268				
29	535	256	279	80-84	652	238	414
				80	176	62	114
30-34	3026	1443	1583	81	162	62	100
30	566	255	311	82	121	44	77
31	601	284	317	83	98	31	67
32	626	311	315	84	95	39	56
33	609	299	310				
34	624	294	330	85-89	316	90	226
				85	84	25	59
35-39	3288	1630	1658	86	76	25	51
35	668	338	330	87	63	18	45
36	685	335	350	88	52	12	40
37	681	341	340	89	41	10	31
38	647	318	329				
39	607	298	309	90 and over	168	23	145
40-44	2865	1399	1466	Under 16	8472	4336	4136
40	593	289	304				
41	607	288	319	Under 18	9532	4903	4629
42	594	295	299				
43	542	270	272	16-44	15817	7753	8064
44	529	257	272				
				45-59/64*	7574	4182	3392
45-49	2443	1249	1194				
45	503	227	276	60/65** and over	5867	2030	3837
46	480	237	243				
47	475	242	233				
48	499	260	239				
49	486	283	203				

*   45 – 64 for males; 45 – 59 for females.
**   65 and over for males; 60 and over for females.

MID-YEAR ESTIMATES

Table M2

Mid-Year Population at 30 June 2001: Resident population by single year of age and sex

Age	All Persons	Males	Females	Age	All Persons	Males	Females
All Ages	66533	31701	34832	50-54	3743	1809	1934
				50	741	371	370
0-4	4302	2187	2115	51	741	376	365
0	795	399	396	52	723	358	365
1	813	399	414	53	726	340	386
2	870	451	419	54	812	364	448
3	886	455	431				
4	938	483	455	55-59	3603	1701	1902
				55	726	351	375
5-9	4647	2390	2257	56	708	327	381
5	890	456	434	57	721	333	388
6	920	468	452	58	734	352	382
7	896	447	449	59	714	338	376
8	930	502	428				
9	1011	517	494	60-64	3142	1471	1671
				60	635	287	348
10-14	4603	2307	2296	61	601	289	312
10	956	455	501	62	637	303	334
11	962	491	471	63	608	292	316
12	925	469	456	64	661	300	361
13	867	445	422				
14	893	447	446	65-69	3036	1351	1685
				65	632	272	360
15-19	3801	1928	1873	66	582	271	311
15	843	429	414	67	574	268	306
16	818	395	423	68	628	263	365
17	755	365	390	69	620	277	343
18	718	379	339				
19	667	360	307	70-74	3016	1313	1703
				70	646	293	353
20-24	3110	1570	1540	71	634	273	361
20	623	339	284	72	613	271	342
21	659	356	303	73	551	240	311
22	627	307	320	74	572	236	336
23	599	288	311				
24	602	280	322	75-79	2411	984	1427
				75	538	217	321
25-29	3902	1865	2037	76	488	203	285
25	650	309	341	77	511	219	292
26	678	318	360	78	450	187	263
27	771	379	392	79	424	158	266
28	878	403	475				
29	925	456	469	80-84	1495	563	932
				80	396	151	245
30-34	5386	2542	2844	81	378	151	227
30	971	457	514	82	280	117	163
31	1011	479	532	83	230	76	154
32	1058	483	575	84	211	68	143
33	1150	543	607				
34	1196	580	616	85-89	693	214	479
				85	196	59	137
35-39	5949	2827	3122	86	168	50	118
35	1169	546	623	87	124	40	84
36	1212	571	641	88	126	41	85
37	1218	577	641	89	79	24	55
38	1197	593	604				
39	1153	540	613	90 and over	325	70	255
40-44	5221	2536	2685	Under 16	14395	7313	7082
40	1147	559	588				
41	1098	538	560	Under 18	15968	8073	7895
42	1053	513	540				
43	980	491	489	16-44	26526	12839	13687
44	943	435	508				
				45-59/64*	12965	7054	5911
45-49	4148	2073	2075				
45	933	449	484	60/65** and over	12647	4495	8152
46	838	415	423				
47	814	422	392				
48	808	404	404				
49	755	383	372				

* 45 – 64 for males; 45 – 59 for females.
** 65 and over for males; 60 and over for females.

MID-YEAR ESTIMATES

Coleraine Local Government District

Table M2

Mid-Year Population at 30 June 2001: Resident population by single year of age and sex

Age	All Persons	Males	Females	Age	All Persons	Males	Females
All Ages	56408	26978	29430	50-54	3403	1661	1742
				50	647	326	321
0-4	3743	1912	1831	51	676	328	348
0	655	352	303	52	688	332	356
1	726	367	359	53	681	332	349
2	771	392	379	54	711	343	368
3	789	393	396				
4	802	408	394	55-59	3100	1552	1548
				55	626	331	295
5-9	3790	1914	1876	56	623	300	323
5	751	380	371	57	625	323	302
6	747	372	375	58	641	306	335
7	757	378	379	59	585	292	293
8	777	401	376				
9	758	383	375	60-64	2833	1303	1530
				60	593	277	316
10-14	4137	2132	2005	61	572	267	305
10	807	407	400	62	553	254	299
11	817	412	405	63	548	256	292
12	843	440	403	64	567	249	318
13	802	416	386				
14	868	457	411	65-69	2386	1125	1261
				65	507	242	265
15-19	4147	2055	2092	66	464	221	243
15	859	456	403	67	462	221	241
16	838	439	399	68	482	234	248
17	783	398	385	69	471	207	264
18	774	376	398				
19	893	386	507	70-74	1968	850	1118
				70	450	191	259
20-24	4025	1795	2230	71	429	185	244
20	951	390	561	72	390	181	209
21	924	416	508	73	338	136	202
22	799	359	440	74	361	157	204
23	698	313	385				
24	653	317	336	75-79	1684	714	970
				75	392	166	226
25-29	3457	1599	1858	76	354	160	194
25	625	299	326	77	322	137	185
26	600	268	332	78	304	126	178
27	691	326	365	79	312	125	187
28	764	344	420				
29	777	362	415	80-84	1120	409	711
				80	273	98	175
30-34	4041	1957	2084	81	251	95	156
30	814	396	418	82	215	76	139
31	746	369	377	83	208	81	127
32	777	375	402	84	173	59	114
33	834	401	433				
34	870	416	454	85-89	606	156	450
				85	135	38	97
35-39	4231	2030	2201	86	128	36	92
35	863	428	435	87	142	37	105
36	874	404	470	88	115	27	88
37	869	420	449	89	86	18	68
38	804	390	414				
39	821	388	433	90 and over	243	60	183
40-44	4008	1998	2010	Under 16	12529	6414	6115
40	811	404	407				
41	814	393	421	Under 18	14150	7251	6899
42	808	406	402				
43	780	378	402	16-44	23050	10978	12072
44	795	417	378				
				45-59/64*	11292	6272	5020
45-49	3486	1756	1730				
45	751	350	401	60/65** and over	9537	3314	6223
46	683	354	329				
47	716	374	342				
48	697	368	329				
49	639	310	329				

*   45 – 64 for males; 45 – 59 for females.
**   65 and over for males; 60 and over for females.

MID-YEAR ESTIMATES

Table M2

Mid-Year Population at 30 June 2001: Resident population by single year of age and sex

Age	All Persons	Males	Females	Age	All Persons	Males	Females
All Ages	32712	16264	16448	50-54	1856	917	939
				50	387	190	197
0-4	2372	1244	1128	51	365	181	184
0	434	249	185	52	358	171	187
1	474	237	237	53	372	181	191
2	482	241	241	54	374	194	180
3	470	252	218				
4	512	265	247	55-59	1678	832	846
				55	353	166	187
5-9	2565	1305	1260	56	352	173	179
5	496	271	225	57	349	180	169
6	520	268	252	58	326	168	158
7	498	251	247	59	298	145	153
8	518	254	264				
9	533	261	272	60-64	1329	643	686
				60	288	154	134
10-14	2903	1484	1419	61	288	137	151
10	568	288	280	62	262	121	141
11	579	298	281	63	254	120	134
12	583	299	284	64	237	111	126
13	584	298	286				
14	589	301	288	65-69	1069	512	557
				65	235	115	120
15-19	2802	1436	1366	66	219	115	104
15	605	319	286	67	215	103	112
16	634	331	303	68	205	96	109
17	602	297	305	69	195	83	112
18	553	275	278				
19	408	214	194	70-74	971	462	509
				70	187	96	91
20-24	2220	1173	1047	71	213	107	106
20	451	237	214	72	210	94	116
21	454	233	221	73	174	80	94
22	434	232	202	74	187	85	102
23	440	231	209				
24	441	240	201	75-79	809	351	458
				75	169	78	91
25-29	2324	1163	1161	76	169	78	91
25	481	238	243	77	180	84	96
26	435	211	224	78	139	52	87
27	454	234	220	79	152	59	93
28	473	239	234				
29	481	241	240	80-84	534	194	340
				80	135	53	82
30-34	2333	1151	1182	81	133	46	87
30	507	255	252	82	110	45	65
31	467	241	226	83	80	26	54
32	433	211	222	84	76	24	52
33	474	230	244				
34	452	214	238	85-89	272	82	190
				85	67	22	45
35-39	2384	1192	1192	86	68	18	50
35	472	219	253	87	49	17	32
36	494	247	247	88	57	17	40
37	503	255	248	89	31	8	23
38	474	263	211				
39	441	208	233	90 and over	110	33	77
40-44	2230	1107	1123	Under 16	8445	4352	4093
40	450	215	235				
41	470	224	246	Under 18	9681	4980	4701
42	430	242	188				
43	438	204	234	16-44	13688	6903	6785
44	442	222	220				
				45-59/64*	6128	3375	2753
45-49	1951	983	968				
45	411	203	208	60/65** and over	4451	1634	2817
46	392	201	191				
47	380	190	190				
48	392	211	181				
49	376	178	198				

* 45 – 64 for males; 45 – 59 for females.
** 65 and over for males; 60 and over for females.

Table M2

Mid-Year Population at 30 June 2001: Resident population by single year of age and sex

Age	All Persons	Males	Females
All Ages	80931	39905	41026
0-4	5736	2971	2765
0	1073	568	505
1	1116	594	522
2	1139	592	547
3	1189	592	597
4	1219	625	594
5-9	6266	3284	2982
5	1201	638	563
6	1206	639	567
7	1266	652	614
8	1292	662	630
9	1301	693	608
10-14	6614	3468	3146
10	1345	718	627
11	1301	690	611
12	1309	699	610
13	1357	695	662
14	1302	666	636
15-19	6050	3117	2933
15	1308	709	599
16	1337	655	682
17	1288	645	643
18	1176	602	574
19	941	506	435
20-24	4699	2340	2359
20	917	476	441
21	974	504	470
22	959	467	492
23	928	450	478
24	921	443	478
25-29	5314	2699	2615
25	988	478	510
26	1012	508	504
27	1036	514	522
28	1102	598	504
29	1176	601	575
30-34	6386	3188	3198
30	1185	584	601
31	1244	650	594
32	1307	664	643
33	1314	652	662
34	1336	638	698
35-39	6520	3241	3279
35	1332	661	671
36	1370	665	705
37	1308	654	654
38	1273	631	642
39	1237	630	607
40-44	5704	2844	2860
40	1193	606	587
41	1238	632	606
42	1106	550	556
43	1113	555	558
44	1054	501	553
45-49	4800	2405	2395
45	990	474	516
46	958	505	453
47	958	480	478
48	987	501	486
49	907	445	462

Age	All Persons	Males	Females
50-54	4679	2307	2372
50	895	468	427
51	946	470	476
52	946	484	462
53	942	444	498
54	950	441	509
55-59	4359	2104	2255
55	904	422	482
56	895	424	471
57	876	439	437
58	912	438	474
59	772	381	391
60-64	3575	1700	1875
60	721	381	340
61	699	341	358
62	738	334	404
63	715	324	391
64	702	320	382
65-69	3139	1455	1684
65	686	334	352
66	641	301	340
67	620	266	354
68	605	285	320
69	587	269	318
70-74	2637	1174	1463
70	573	252	321
71	563	263	300
72	523	234	289
73	504	216	288
74	474	209	265
75-79	2089	817	1272
75	460	188	272
76	443	171	272
77	428	182	246
78	400	151	249
79	358	125	233
80-84	1370	511	859
80	359	138	221
81	329	128	201
82	284	108	176
83	205	68	137
84	193	69	124
85-89	703	221	482
85	196	66	130
86	155	48	107
87	140	43	97
88	116	36	80
89	96	28	68
90 and over	291	59	232
Under 16	19924	10432	9492
Under 18	22549	11732	10817
16-44	33365	16720	16645
45-59/64*	15538	8516	7022
60/65** and over	12104	4237	7867

* 45 – 64 for males; 45 – 59 for females.
** 65 and over for males; 60 and over for females.

Table M2

Mid-Year Population at 30 June 2001: Resident population by single year of age and sex

Age	All Persons	Males	Females	Age	All Persons	Males	Females
All Ages	105335	51355	53980	50-54	5669	2820	2849
				50	1175	565	610
0-4	8060	4193	3867	51	1163	590	573
0	1505	791	714	52	1125	578	547
1	1538	815	723	53	1105	534	571
2	1614	827	787	54	1101	553	548
3	1670	876	794				
4	1733	884	849	55-59	4766	2321	2445
				55	999	506	493
5-9	8570	4305	4265	56	942	446	496
5	1735	884	851	57	1023	487	536
6	1668	846	822	58	976	472	504
7	1659	839	820	59	826	410	416
8	1756	860	896				
9	1752	876	876	60-64	3983	1961	2022
				60	826	409	417
10-14	9588	4875	4713	61	779	376	403
10	1839	917	922	62	790	381	409
11	1827	929	898	63	807	419	388
12	1895	971	924	64	781	376	405
13	2036	1034	1002				
14	1991	1024	967	65-69	3327	1536	1791
				65	746	345	401
15-19	9428	4934	4494	66	690	331	359
15	1943	1036	907	67	636	291	345
16	1967	1030	937	68	640	290	350
17	1996	1027	969	69	615	279	336
18	1854	964	890				
19	1668	877	791	70-74	2790	1236	1554
				70	623	282	341
20-24	7710	3860	3850	71	552	245	307
20	1608	813	795	72	578	246	332
21	1619	823	796	73	529	235	294
22	1520	747	773	74	508	228	280
23	1472	718	754				
24	1491	759	732	75-79	2052	772	1280
				75	490	197	293
25-29	7566	3636	3930	76	440	169	271
25	1481	726	755	77	397	155	242
26	1482	716	766	78	369	130	239
27	1512	730	782	79	356	121	235
28	1541	729	812				
29	1550	735	815	80-84	1255	443	812
				80	337	118	219
30-34	8216	3953	4263	81	301	105	196
30	1604	761	843	82	245	93	152
31	1620	784	836	83	202	74	128
32	1667	825	842	84	170	53	117
33	1684	803	881				
34	1641	780	861	85-89	641	171	470
				85	170	60	110
35-39	8233	3939	4294	86	144	45	99
35	1690	778	912	87	127	25	102
36	1690	824	866	88	103	18	85
37	1611	788	823	89	97	23	74
38	1635	769	866				
39	1607	780	827	90 and over	271	60	211
40-44	7136	3421	3715	Under 16	28161	14409	13752
40	1583	763	820				
41	1489	726	763	Under 18	32124	16466	15658
42	1396	667	729				
43	1369	651	718	16-44	46346	22707	23639
44	1299	614	685				
				45-59/64*	18470	10021	8449
45-49	6074	2919	3155				
45	1278	618	660	60/65** and over	12358	4218	8140
46	1275	639	636				
47	1226	570	656				
48	1165	556	609				
49	1130	536	594				

* 45 – 64 for males; 45 – 59 for females.
** 65 and over for males; 60 and over for females.

Table M2

Mid-Year Population at 30 June 2001: Resident population by single year of age and sex

Age	All Persons	Males	Females	Age	All Persons	Males	Females
All Ages	64147	31844	32303	50-54	3867	1954	1913
				50	785	391	394
0-4	4434	2287	2147	51	799	405	394
0	861	430	431	52	758	385	373
1	837	445	392	53	801	414	387
2	874	463	411	54	724	359	365
3	936	494	442				
4	926	455	471	55-59	3371	1707	1664
				55	709	354	355
5-9	5004	2549	2455	56	697	357	340
5	964	499	465	57	684	332	352
6	965	509	456	58	685	354	331
7	991	483	508	59	596	310	286
8	1013	494	519				
9	1071	564	507	60-64	2770	1347	1423
				60	589	280	309
10-14	5317	2711	2606	61	545	270	275
10	1064	551	513	62	558	286	272
11	1081	555	526	63	530	253	277
12	1041	520	521	64	548	258	290
13	1066	552	514				
14	1065	533	532	65-69	2401	1123	1278
				65	517	245	272
15-19	5208	2716	2492	66	504	250	254
15	1089	567	522	67	482	232	250
16	1115	569	546	68	480	211	269
17	1057	551	506	69	418	185	233
18	1050	543	507				
19	897	486	411	70-74	2006	885	1121
				70	422	199	223
20-24	3942	2138	1804	71	420	194	226
20	820	469	351	72	397	177	220
21	794	450	344	73	395	163	232
22	796	414	382	74	372	152	220
23	786	409	377				
24	746	396	350	75-79	1683	664	1019
				75	363	141	222
25-29	3974	2044	1930	76	367	145	222
25	782	417	365	77	334	135	199
26	740	382	358	78	308	123	185
27	760	384	376	79	311	120	191
28	840	421	419				
29	852	440	412	80-84	1121	450	671
				80	289	128	161
30-34	4706	2347	2359	81	274	117	157
30	924	463	461	82	196	78	118
31	885	429	456	83	192	68	124
32	980	484	496	84	170	59	111
33	960	470	490				
34	957	501	456	85-89	617	179	438
				85	147	53	94
35-39	5009	2494	2515	86	137	33	104
35	1025	515	510	87	123	34	89
36	1034	506	528	88	107	27	80
37	992	488	504	89	103	32	71
38	961	491	470				
39	997	494	503	90 and over	325	77	248
40-44	4418	2202	2216	Under 16	15844	8114	7730
40	879	430	449				
41	913	467	446	Under 18	18016	9234	8782
42	893	442	451				
43	901	441	460	16-44	26168	13374	12794
44	832	422	410				
				45-59/64*	12559	6978	5581
45-49	3974	1970	2004				
45	853	419	434	60/65** and over	9576	3378	6198
46	796	393	403				
47	817	405	412				
48	755	378	377	* 45 – 64 for males; 45 – 59 for females.			
49	753	375	378	** 65 and over for males; 60 and over for females.			

MID-YEAR ESTIMATES

Table M2

Mid-Year Population at 30 June 2001: Resident population by single year of age and sex

Age	All Persons	Males	Females	Age	All Persons	Males	Females
All Ages	47849	23685	24164	50-54	2702	1329	1373
				50	544	271	273
0-4	3557	1816	1741	51	539	261	278
0	647	341	306	52	552	281	271
1	717	361	356	53	548	265	283
2	739	350	389	54	519	251	268
3	715	382	333				
4	739	382	357	55-59	2351	1173	1178
				55	503	257	246
5-9	3746	1908	1838	56	481	226	255
5	709	354	355	57	475	236	239
6	723	386	337	58	452	236	216
7	749	385	364	59	440	218	222
8	757	388	369				
9	808	395	413	60-64	2008	978	1030
				60	420	191	229
10-14	4133	2086	2047	61	400	207	193
10	827	414	413	62	419	197	222
11	821	420	401	63	384	193	191
12	815	414	401	64	385	190	195
13	787	374	413				
14	883	464	419	65-69	1808	852	956
				65	387	196	191
15-19	3937	2006	1931	66	349	165	184
15	850	444	406	67	338	163	175
16	827	426	401	68	376	162	214
17	868	435	433	69	358	166	192
18	802	392	410				
19	590	309	281	70-74	1580	673	907
				70	364	147	217
20-24	3023	1564	1459	71	310	134	176
20	550	306	244	72	295	138	157
21	596	322	274	73	329	133	196
22	635	334	301	74	282	121	161
23	594	306	288				
24	648	296	352	75-79	1246	518	728
				75	272	121	151
25-29	3450	1734	1716	76	289	119	170
25	673	340	333	77	240	103	137
26	637	337	300	78	237	92	145
27	705	355	350	79	208	83	125
28	751	368	383				
29	684	334	350	80-84	778	284	494
				80	201	68	133
30-34	3501	1794	1707	81	170	66	104
30	747	409	338	82	144	61	83
31	681	360	321	83	126	44	82
32	676	314	362	84	137	45	92
33	708	358	350				
34	689	353	336	85-89	392	119	273
				85	106	29	77
35-39	3382	1686	1696	86	93	32	61
35	701	348	353	87	80	22	58
36	666	336	330	88	65	22	43
37	678	332	346	89	48	14	34
38	659	326	333				
39	678	344	334	90 and over	184	49	135
40-44	3226	1637	1589	Under 16	12286	6254	6032
40	693	356	337				
41	679	350	329	Under 18	13981	7115	6866
42	619	313	306				
43	620	310	310	16-44	19669	9977	9692
44	615	308	307				
				45-59/64*	8876	4959	3917
45-49	2845	1479	1366				
45	606	311	295	60/65** and over	7018	2495	4523
46	594	313	281				
47	584	305	279				
48	528	264	264	* 45 – 64 for males; 45 – 59 for females.			
49	533	286	247	** 65 and over for males; 60 and over for females.			

MID-YEAR ESTIMATES

Table M2

Mid-Year Population at 30 June 2001: Resident population by single year of age and sex

Age	All Persons	Males	Females		Age	All Persons	Males	Females
All Ages	57687	28899	28788		50-54	3594	1799	1795
					50	716	367	349
0-4	3903	1969	1934		51	691	350	341
0	733	385	348		52	756	362	394
1	736	357	379		53	703	351	352
2	808	412	396		54	728	369	359
3	814	396	418					
4	812	419	393		55-59	2984	1526	1458
					55	626	333	293
5-9	4087	2184	1903		56	606	306	300
5	811	434	377		57	611	331	280
6	792	421	371		58	593	283	310
7	848	458	390		59	548	273	275
8	824	443	381					
9	812	428	384		60-64	2453	1262	1191
					60	471	240	231
10-14	4756	2433	2323		61	493	260	233
10	912	466	446		62	498	266	232
11	931	461	470		63	484	244	240
12	970	488	482		64	507	252	255
13	939	512	427					
14	1004	506	498		65-69	2224	1070	1154
					65	455	213	242
15-19	4832	2424	2408		66	449	218	231
15	1061	525	536		67	470	224	246
16	1044	520	524		68	419	201	218
17	1062	533	529		69	431	214	217
18	972	479	493					
19	693	367	326		70-74	1964	911	1053
					70	391	188	203
20-24	3299	1752	1547		71	390	186	204
20	647	349	298		72	403	190	213
21	611	351	260		73	370	159	211
22	689	365	324		74	410	188	222
23	682	351	331					
24	670	336	334		75-79	1727	716	1011
					75	382	174	208
25-29	3752	1921	1831		76	347	140	207
25	682	343	339		77	360	145	215
26	698	353	345		78	344	136	208
27	747	381	366		79	294	121	173
28	796	409	387					
29	829	435	394		80-84	1143	450	693
					80	269	116	153
30-34	4036	2056	1980		81	257	100	157
30	826	416	410		82	238	97	141
31	827	409	418		83	197	78	119
32	803	411	392		84	182	59	123
33	796	412	384					
34	784	408	376		85-89	637	219	418
					85	164	50	114
35-39	4168	2123	2045		86	137	44	93
35	807	393	414		87	126	45	81
36	864	458	406		88	118	47	71
37	862	437	425		89	92	33	59
38	834	423	411					
39	801	412	389		90 and over	259	74	185
40-44	4038	2018	2020		Under 16	13807	7111	6696
40	832	415	417					
41	820	408	412		Under 18	15913	8164	7749
42	781	378	403					
43	822	412	410		16-44	23064	11769	11295
44	783	405	378					
					45-59/64*	11671	6579	5092
45-49	3831	1992	1839					
45	822	430	392		60/65** and over	9145	3440	5705
46	767	402	365					
47	767	401	366					
48	738	377	361		* 45 – 64 for males; 45 – 59 for females.			
49	737	382	355		** 65 and over for males; 60 and over for females.			

MID-YEAR ESTIMATES

Table M2

Mid-Year Population at 30 June 2001: Resident population by single year of age and sex

Age	All Persons	Males	Females	Age	All Persons	Males	Females
All Ages	30811	15118	15693	50-54	2035	995	1040
				50	397	192	205
0-4	1869	970	899	51	397	183	214
0	330	159	171	52	386	193	193
1	382	200	182	53	412	204	208
2	380	200	180	54	443	223	220
3	367	200	167				
4	410	211	199	55-59	1854	943	911
				55	377	198	179
5-9	2092	1047	1045	56	345	180	165
5	401	204	197	57	386	188	198
6	391	208	183	58	402	207	195
7	407	207	200	59	344	170	174
8	437	213	224				
9	456	215	241	60-64	1544	746	798
				60	313	153	160
10-14	2259	1197	1062	61	314	148	166
10	459	248	211	62	310	158	152
11	434	232	202	63	298	153	145
12	458	249	209	64	309	134	175
13	466	240	226				
14	442	228	214	65-69	1390	667	723
				65	281	128	153
15-19	2108	1041	1067	66	293	130	163
15	452	217	235	67	272	138	134
16	443	215	228	68	289	137	152
17	462	232	230	69	255	134	121
18	406	200	206				
19	345	177	168	70-74	1150	501	649
				70	273	125	148
20-24	1536	754	782	71	239	104	135
20	317	158	159	72	219	95	124
21	314	154	160	73	210	86	124
22	307	152	155	74	209	91	118
23	294	134	160				
24	304	156	148	75-79	912	382	530
				75	202	90	112
25-29	1817	880	937	76	178	80	98
25	302	155	147	77	183	76	107
26	356	169	187	78	171	69	102
27	365	190	175	79	178	67	111
28	390	185	205				
29	404	181	223	80-84	651	248	403
				80	159	66	93
30-34	2303	1137	1166	81	155	61	94
30	424	205	219	82	146	48	98
31	466	234	232	83	101	39	62
32	459	228	231	84	90	34	56
33	465	232	233				
34	489	238	251	85-89	316	78	238
				85	76	31	45
35-39	2524	1236	1288	86	82	18	64
35	483	233	250	87	61	11	50
36	504	248	256	88	50	11	39
37	523	251	272	89	47	7	40
38	517	258	259				
39	497	246	251	90 and over	147	29	118
40-44	2361	1233	1128	Under 16	6672	3431	3241
40	485	276	209				
41	486	252	234	Under 18	7577	3878	3699
42	483	244	239				
43	476	246	230	16-44	12197	6064	6133
44	431	215	216				
				45-59/64*	6578	3718	2860
45-49	1943	1034	909				
45	418	210	208	60/65** and over	5364	1905	3459
46	383	211	172				
47	369	218	151				
48	383	188	195				
49	390	207	183				

* 45 – 64 for males; 45 – 59 for females.
** 65 and over for males; 60 and over for females.

MID-YEAR ESTIMATES

Table M2

Mid-Year Population at 30 June 2001: Resident population by single year of age and sex

Age	All Persons	Males	Females		Age	All Persons	Males	Females
All Ages	32639	16698	15941		50-54	1782	904	878
					50	375	186	189
0-4	2457	1242	1215		51	369	183	186
0	463	222	241		52	363	190	173
1	468	240	228		53	327	173	154
2	513	251	262		54	348	172	176
3	490	234	256					
4	523	295	228		55-59	1583	765	818
					55	341	158	183
5-9	2579	1336	1243		56	344	178	166
5	518	278	240		57	325	165	160
6	531	264	267		58	294	129	165
7	488	254	234		59	279	135	144
8	495	258	237					
9	547	282	265		60-64	1266	652	614
					60	271	142	129
10-14	2686	1410	1276		61	229	124	105
10	553	297	256		62	278	140	138
11	533	295	238		63	247	126	121
12	530	270	260		64	241	120	121
13	533	268	265					
14	537	280	257		65-69	946	459	487
					65	202	101	101
15-19	2646	1379	1267		66	187	90	97
15	554	291	263		67	178	80	98
16	512	253	259		68	182	89	93
17	548	287	261		69	197	99	98
18	550	287	263					
19	482	261	221		70-74	847	382	465
					70	174	91	83
20-24	2300	1254	1046		71	175	83	92
20	429	233	196		72	178	74	104
21	443	248	195		73	170	72	98
22	432	240	192		74	150	62	88
23	473	244	229					
24	523	289	234		75-79	676	268	408
					75	154	64	90
25-29	2703	1426	1277		76	124	52	72
25	530	281	249		77	145	59	86
26	513	268	245		78	136	49	87
27	542	285	257		79	117	44	73
28	550	292	258					
29	568	300	268		80-84	411	166	245
					80	108	50	58
30-34	2724	1432	1292		81	95	40	55
30	557	292	265		82	95	38	57
31	537	280	257		83	59	16	43
32	554	278	276		84	54	22	32
33	542	293	249					
34	534	289	245		85-89	218	69	149
					85	54	17	37
35-39	2593	1369	1224		86	50	17	33
35	574	313	261		87	51	16	35
36	572	296	276		88	38	12	26
37	496	257	239		89	25	7	18
38	482	263	219					
39	469	240	229		90 and over	85	23	62
40-44	2133	1103	1030		Under 16	8276	4279	3997
40	474	247	227					
41	438	223	215		Under 18	9336	4819	4517
42	426	203	223					
43	400	211	189		16-44	14545	7672	6873
44	395	219	176					
45-49	2004	1059	945		45-59/64*	6021	3380	2641
45	394	216	178					
46	456	254	202		60/65** and over	3797	1367	2430
47	401	208	193					
48	383	205	178					
49	370	176	194					

*   45 – 64 for males; 45 – 59 for females.
** 65 and over for males; 60 and over for females.

MID-YEAR ESTIMATES

73

Table M2

Mid-Year Population at 30 June 2001: Resident population by single year of age and sex

Age	All Persons	Males	Females	Age	All Persons	Males	Females
All Ages	108997	53235	55762	50-54	6454	3153	3301
				50	1218	615	603
0-4	7748	4038	3710	51	1264	633	631
0	1417	721	696	52	1349	643	706
1	1490	789	701	53	1323	627	696
2	1566	787	779	54	1300	635	665
3	1592	837	755				
4	1683	904	779	55-59	5745	2811	2934
				55	1140	576	564
5-9	8564	4452	4112	56	1187	589	598
5	1727	913	814	57	1199	567	632
6	1693	881	812	58	1205	575	630
7	1638	850	788	59	1014	504	510
8	1717	876	841				
9	1789	932	857	60-64	4589	2180	2409
				60	960	469	491
10-14	8633	4428	4205	61	959	450	509
10	1770	904	866	62	961	450	511
11	1746	882	864	63	864	416	448
12	1702	866	836	64	845	395	450
13	1712	897	815				
14	1703	879	824	65-69	3982	1863	2119
				65	844	407	437
15-19	8130	4136	3994	66	809	390	419
15	1676	848	828	67	789	370	419
16	1749	899	850	68	767	348	419
17	1685	839	846	69	773	348	425
18	1600	814	786				
19	1420	736	684	70-74	3365	1466	1899
				70	723	346	377
20-24	6578	3345	3233	71	683	292	391
20	1392	746	646	72	679	281	398
21	1328	742	586	73	635	257	378
22	1315	648	667	74	645	290	355
23	1228	577	651				
24	1315	632	683	75-79	2583	1047	1536
				75	608	256	352
25-29	7121	3538	3583	76	539	224	315
25	1305	661	644	77	504	201	303
26	1344	689	655	78	467	179	288
27	1418	689	729	79	465	187	278
28	1490	720	770				
29	1564	779	785	80-84	1692	606	1086
				80	464	177	287
30-34	8726	4243	4483	81	414	164	250
30	1681	825	856	82	325	108	217
31	1674	796	878	83	252	80	172
32	1744	838	906	84	237	77	160
33	1770	875	895				
34	1857	909	948	85-89	888	254	634
				85	231	60	171
35-39	9047	4367	4680	86	179	54	125
35	1826	916	910	87	182	57	125
36	1876	910	966	88	174	52	122
37	1786	849	937	89	122	31	91
38	1790	849	941				
39	1769	843	926	90 and over	431	76	355
40-44	7964	3848	4116	Under 16	26621	13766	12855
40	1750	831	919				
41	1631	782	849	Under 18	30055	15504	14551
42	1547	746	801				
43	1560	764	796	16-44	45890	22629	23261
44	1476	725	751				
				45-59/64*	21136	11528	9608
45-49	6757	3384	3373				
45	1481	760	721	60/65** and over	15350	5312	10038
46	1354	693	661				
47	1345	690	655				
48	1307	628	679	* 45 – 64 for males; 45 – 59 for females.			
49	1270	613	657	** 65 and over for males; 60 and over for females.			

Magherafelt Local Government District

Table M2

Mid-Year Population at 30 June 2001: Resident population by single year of age and sex

Age	All Persons	Males	Females
All Ages	39891	20076	19815
0-4	3022	1563	1459
0	551	291	260
1	614	311	303
2	603	302	301
3	645	346	299
4	609	313	296
5-9	3167	1600	1567
5	663	341	322
6	625	317	308
7	620	311	309
8	614	320	294
9	645	311	334
10-14	3443	1767	1676
10	643	327	316
11	686	335	351
12	721	385	336
13	695	365	330
14	698	355	343
15-19	3213	1649	1564
15	703	353	350
16	690	365	325
17	674	330	344
18	661	337	324
19	485	264	221
20-24	2730	1465	1265
20	467	235	232
21	503	252	251
22	618	356	262
23	568	312	256
24	574	310	264
25-29	3131	1651	1480
25	627	346	281
26	582	299	283
27	695	393	302
28	603	302	301
29	624	311	313
30-34	3153	1630	1523
30	659	352	307
31	659	336	323
32	628	316	312
33	619	312	307
34	588	314	274
35-39	2944	1501	1443
35	617	314	303
36	592	305	287
37	605	299	306
38	572	302	270
39	558	281	277
40-44	2637	1283	1354
40	563	263	300
41	523	258	265
42	516	254	262
43	525	254	271
44	510	254	256
45-49	2327	1201	1126
45	483	244	239
46	463	229	234
47	487	266	221
48	448	239	209
49	446	223	223
50-54	2147	1077	1070
50	461	238	223
51	429	212	217
52	404	191	213
53	418	224	194
54	435	212	223
55-59	1887	922	965
55	402	204	198
56	410	195	215
57	373	188	185
58	360	179	181
59	342	156	186
60-64	1517	733	784
60	314	165	149
61	333	160	173
62	312	139	173
63	278	123	155
64	280	146	134
65-69	1385	673	712
65	284	142	142
66	274	130	144
67	292	150	142
68	273	127	146
69	262	124	138
70-74	1183	544	639
70	261	119	142
71	258	126	132
72	217	104	113
73	224	102	122
74	223	93	130
75-79	911	395	516
75	209	97	112
76	190	94	96
77	176	71	105
78	172	60	112
79	164	73	91
80-84	656	269	387
80	150	69	81
81	167	68	99
82	128	48	80
83	111	47	64
84	100	37	63
85-89	320	112	208
85	77	28	49
86	74	23	51
87	69	21	48
88	50	20	30
89	50	20	30
90 and over	118	41	77
Under 16	10335	5283	5052
Under 18	11699	5978	5721
16-44	17105	8826	8279
45-59/64*	7094	3933	3161
60/65** and over	5357	2034	3323

*   45 – 64 for males; 45 – 59 for females.
** 65 and over for males; 60 and over for females.

MID-YEAR ESTIMATES

75

Table M2

Mid-Year Population at 30 June 2001: Resident population by single year of age and sex

Age	All Persons	Males	Females	Age	All Persons	Males	Females
All Ages	15961	7841	8120	50-54	995	524	471
				50	212	110	102
0-4	1093	568	525	51	208	117	91
0	198	97	101	52	182	94	88
1	206	108	98	53	195	98	97
2	233	127	106	54	198	105	93
3	219	116	103				
4	237	120	117	55-59	917	447	470
				55	196	91	105
5-9	1084	544	540	56	186	88	98
5	200	108	92	57	192	91	101
6	207	104	103	58	175	90	85
7	216	96	120	59	168	87	81
8	226	117	109				
9	235	119	116	60-64	816	389	427
				60	154	73	81
10-14	1300	668	632	61	151	75	76
10	255	129	126	62	163	74	89
11	258	135	123	63	167	76	91
12	250	122	128	64	181	91	90
13	260	136	124				
14	277	146	131	65-69	656	331	325
				65	158	81	77
15-19	1274	663	611	66	132	70	62
15	292	142	150	67	121	55	66
16	279	154	125	68	124	58	66
17	262	129	133	69	121	67	54
18	240	131	109				
19	201	107	94	70-74	577	246	331
				70	123	55	68
20-24	858	427	431	71	126	59	67
20	192	95	97	72	104	43	61
21	169	84	85	73	111	42	69
22	183	91	92	74	113	47	66
23	156	84	72				
24	158	73	85	75-79	511	194	317
				75	125	48	77
25-29	980	470	510	76	98	32	66
25	182	88	94	77	107	39	68
26	191	87	104	78	91	37	54
27	189	88	101	79	90	38	52
28	205	107	98				
29	213	100	113	80-84	315	128	187
				80	75	31	44
30-34	1083	557	526	81	64	25	39
30	209	107	102	82	63	26	37
31	222	119	103	83	57	23	34
32	226	123	103	84	56	23	33
33	216	103	113				
34	210	105	105	85-89	182	65	117
				85	42	16	26
35-39	1096	520	576	86	47	19	28
35	203	92	111	87	42	13	29
36	226	102	124	88	30	9	21
37	234	113	121	89	21	8	13
38	224	111	113				
39	209	102	107	90 and over	71	7	64
40-44	1093	530	563	Under 16	3769	1922	1847
40	228	123	105				
41	217	117	100	Under 18	4310	2205	2105
42	219	104	115				
43	219	101	118	16-44	6092	3025	3067
44	210	85	125				
				45-59/64*	3361	1923	1438
45-49	1060	563	497				
45	193	97	96	60/65** and over	2739	971	1768
46	213	112	101				
47	202	112	90				
48	224	114	110				
49	228	128	100				

*   45 – 64 for males; 45 – 59 for females.
** 65 and over for males; 60 and over for females.

MID-YEAR ESTIMATES

Table M2

Mid-Year Population at 30 June 2001: Resident population by single year of age and sex

Age	All Persons	Males	Females		Age	All Persons	Males	Females
All Ages	87399	43258	44141		50-54	4809	2392	2417
					50	961	458	503
0-4	6828	3499	3329		51	984	484	500
0	1312	695	617		52	1011	500	511
1	1324	678	646		53	933	480	453
2	1363	675	688		54	920	470	450
3	1423	748	675					
4	1406	703	703		55-59	4130	2037	2093
					55	879	428	451
5-9	7075	3669	3406		56	878	448	430
5	1417	753	664		57	848	421	427
6	1412	748	664		58	804	379	425
7	1373	712	661		59	721	361	360
8	1413	714	699					
9	1460	742	718		60-64	3502	1745	1757
					60	707	337	370
10-14	7750	4011	3739		61	745	388	357
10	1540	808	732		62	673	345	328
11	1534	808	726		63	661	327	334
12	1527	798	729		64	716	348	368
13	1576	795	781					
14	1573	802	771		65-69	3207	1521	1686
					65	715	346	369
15-19	7289	3691	3598		66	674	329	345
15	1535	761	774		67	637	301	336
16	1538	761	777		68	606	280	326
17	1558	781	777		69	575	265	310
18	1505	781	724					
19	1153	607	546		70-74	2632	1122	1510
					70	542	228	314
20-24	5651	2904	2747		71	559	249	310
20	1039	555	484		72	526	230	296
21	1148	594	554		73	490	208	282
22	1114	548	566		74	515	207	308
23	1157	591	566					
24	1193	616	577		75-79	2140	902	1238
					75	477	197	280
25-29	5778	2854	2924		76	445	187	258
25	1090	559	531		77	422	183	239
26	1088	568	520		78	412	182	230
27	1145	562	583		79	384	153	231
28	1183	578	605					
29	1272	587	685		80-84	1281	466	815
					80	341	119	222
30-34	6493	3178	3315		81	298	107	191
30	1332	660	672		82	242	92	150
31	1275	595	680		83	212	78	134
32	1288	624	664		84	188	70	118
33	1332	662	670					
34	1266	637	629		85-89	675	207	468
					85	196	77	119
35-39	6611	3350	3261		86	164	42	122
35	1336	690	646		87	124	39	85
36	1364	702	662		88	98	26	72
37	1369	683	686		89	93	23	70
38	1329	668	661					
39	1213	607	606		90 and over	269	53	216
40-44	6009	2993	3016		Under 16	23188	11940	11248
40	1304	658	646					
41	1233	595	638		Under 18	26284	13482	12802
42	1138	577	561					
43	1159	565	594		16-44	36296	18209	18087
44	1175	598	577					
					45-59/64*	15954	8838	7116
45-49	5270	2664	2606					
45	1081	551	530		60/65** and over	11961	4271	7690
46	1078	547	531					
47	1064	547	517					
48	1051	530	521					
49	996	489	507					

*   45 – 64 for males; 45 – 59 for females.
** 65 and over for males; 60 and over for females.

Table M2

Mid-Year Population at 30 June 2001: Resident population by single year of age and sex

Age	All Persons	Males	Females	Age	All Persons	Males	Females
All Ages	80144	38758	41386	50-54	4876	2364	2512
				50	983	478	505
0-4	5069	2651	2418	51	940	460	480
0	953	519	434	52	977	478	499
1	963	490	473	53	968	480	488
2	1005	518	487	54	1008	468	540
3	1064	548	516				
4	1084	576	508	55-59	4537	2229	2308
				55	925	450	475
5-9	5482	2848	2634	56	928	449	479
5	1028	537	491	57	948	473	475
6	1093	581	512	58	910	458	452
7	1105	556	549	59	826	399	427
8	1109	567	542				
9	1147	607	540	60-64	3812	1799	2013
				60	747	368	379
10-14	5646	2891	2755	61	734	327	407
10	1158	586	572	62	804	388	416
11	1103	590	513	63	762	356	406
12	1114	552	562	64	765	360	405
13	1160	589	571				
14	1111	574	537	65-69	3410	1602	1808
				65	730	348	382
15-19	5516	2727	2789	66	698	335	363
15	1130	567	563	67	675	313	362
16	1144	564	580	68	630	294	336
17	1069	515	554	69	677	312	365
18	1017	507	510				
19	1156	574	582	70-74	3160	1404	1756
				70	673	302	371
20-24	5001	2469	2532	71	628	286	342
20	1022	521	501	72	628	280	348
21	984	503	481	73	624	266	358
22	998	502	496	74	607	270	337
23	997	478	519				
24	1000	465	535	75-79	2374	965	1409
				75	566	234	332
25-29	5445	2630	2815	76	504	208	296
25	995	490	505	77	461	189	272
26	1072	496	576	78	420	170	250
27	1085	531	554	79	423	164	259
28	1126	563	563				
29	1167	550	617	80-84	1359	499	860
				80	375	145	230
30-34	6216	3017	3199	81	329	122	207
30	1261	625	636	82	252	96	156
31	1202	591	611	83	216	74	142
32	1242	609	633	84	187	62	125
33	1223	569	654				
34	1288	623	665	85-89	715	185	530
				85	190	56	134
35-39	6382	3114	3268	86	153	36	117
35	1268	641	627	87	147	31	116
36	1290	616	674	88	118	33	85
37	1313	617	696	89	107	29	78
38	1273	640	633				
39	1238	600	638	90 and over	331	64	267
40-44	5781	2776	3005	Under 16	17327	8957	8370
40	1216	567	649				
41	1155	546	609	Under 18	19540	10036	9504
42	1128	547	581				
43	1199	590	609	16-44	33211	16166	17045
44	1083	526	557				
				45-59/64*	16244	8916	7328
45-49	5032	2524	2508				
45	1065	542	523	60/65** and over	13362	4719	8643
46	989	501	488				
47	1009	518	491				
48	1003	491	512				
49	966	472	494				

* 45 – 64 for males; 45 – 59 for females.
** 65 and over for males; 60 and over for females.

MID-YEAR ESTIMATES

North Down Local Government District

Table M2

Mid-Year Population at 30 June 2001: Resident population by single year of age and sex

Age	All Persons	Males	Females	Age	All Persons	Males	Females
All Ages	76578	37080	39498	50-54	5452	2635	2817
				50	1034	508	526
0-4	4228	2169	2059	51	1045	520	525
0	758	381	377	52	1109	528	581
1	862	437	425	53	1137	531	606
2	865	443	422	54	1127	548	579
3	872	460	412				
4	871	448	423	55-59	5023	2454	2569
				55	1030	503	527
5-9	4627	2387	2240	56	1030	489	541
5	905	485	420	57	1117	550	567
6	888	457	431	58	982	480	502
7	924	486	438	59	864	432	432
8	903	449	454				
9	1007	510	497	60-64	3547	1713	1834
				60	732	358	374
10-14	5141	2604	2537	61	703	342	361
10	1073	570	503	62	716	340	376
11	961	476	485	63	701	336	365
12	1004	495	509	64	695	337	358
13	1029	525	504				
14	1074	538	536	65-69	3269	1520	1749
				65	700	335	365
15-19	5281	2767	2514	66	685	327	358
15	1087	563	524	67	618	284	334
16	1078	540	538	68	637	298	339
17	1124	583	541	69	629	276	353
18	1058	578	480				
19	934	503	431	70-74	2971	1281	1690
				70	612	277	335
20-24	4322	2272	2050	71	612	259	353
20	873	488	385	72	594	257	337
21	936	504	432	73	567	247	320
22	853	450	403	74	586	241	345
23	848	425	423				
24	812	405	407	75-79	2678	1025	1653
				75	586	228	358
25-29	4607	2404	2203	76	558	227	331
25	837	443	394	77	514	202	312
26	885	457	428	78	513	178	335
27	917	474	443	79	507	190	317
28	962	495	467				
29	1006	535	471	80-84	1952	691	1261
				80	499	188	311
30-34	5455	2713	2742	81	466	175	291
30	1036	536	500	82	366	138	228
31	1106	554	552	83	315	98	217
32	1109	545	564	84	306	92	214
33	1091	539	552				
34	1113	539	574	85-89	1140	321	819
				85	277	78	199
35-39	5687	2772	2915	86	263	78	185
35	1074	522	552	87	228	62	166
36	1156	566	590	88	191	57	134
37	1155	565	590	89	181	46	135
38	1167	552	615				
39	1135	567	568	90 and over	537	136	401
40-44	5470	2628	2842	Under 16	15083	7723	7360
40	1140	546	594				
41	1086	535	551	Under 18	17285	8846	8439
42	1066	503	563				
43	1112	525	587	16-44	29735	14993	14742
44	1066	519	547				
				45-59/64*	17379	9390	7989
45-49	5191	2588	2603				
45	1048	532	516	60/65** and over	14381	4974	9407
46	1004	498	506				
47	1053	524	529				
48	1042	506	536	* 45 – 64 for males; 45 – 59 for females.			
49	1044	528	516	** 65 and over for males; 60 and over for females.			

MID-YEAR ESTIMATES

Table M2

Mid-Year Population at 30 June 2001: Resident population by single year of age and sex

Age	All Persons	Males	Females	Age	All Persons	Males	Females
All Ages	48109	24178	23931	50-54	2632	1358	1274
				50	541	286	255
0-4	3570	1830	1740	51	560	292	268
0	669	333	336	52	540	269	271
1	719	369	350	53	492	248	244
2	714	368	346	54	499	263	236
3	730	382	348				
4	738	378	360	55-59	2254	1127	1127
				55	484	245	239
5-9	3829	1916	1913	56	469	230	239
5	777	401	376	57	458	233	225
6	764	382	382	58	441	228	213
7	798	394	404	59	402	191	211
8	747	373	374				
9	743	366	377	60-64	1870	904	966
				60	412	192	220
10-14	4058	2104	1954	61	397	188	209
10	771	406	365	62	387	189	198
11	808	414	394	63	336	175	161
12	788	410	378	64	338	160	178
13	836	437	399				
14	855	437	418	65-69	1636	809	827
				65	360	174	186
15-19	4143	2171	1972	66	307	167	140
15	877	435	442	67	327	156	171
16	876	455	421	68	321	158	163
17	919	465	454	69	321	154	167
18	845	452	393				
19	626	364	262	70-74	1386	621	765
				70	286	135	151
20-24	3216	1783	1433	71	287	130	157
20	626	373	253	72	262	105	157
21	630	366	264	73	270	113	157
22	645	345	300	74	281	138	143
23	688	378	310				
24	627	321	306	75-79	1145	472	673
				75	232	100	132
25-29	3474	1759	1715	76	242	107	135
25	618	333	285	77	232	100	132
26	673	327	346	78	235	89	146
27	685	351	334	79	204	76	128
28	755	366	389				
29	743	382	361	80-84	763	291	472
				80	189	77	112
30-34	3573	1828	1745	81	179	69	110
30	734	388	346	82	156	61	95
31	731	376	355	83	126	42	84
32	729	344	385	84	113	42	71
33	716	362	354				
34	663	358	305	85-89	439	145	294
				85	112	41	71
35-39	3510	1783	1727	86	110	38	72
35	684	351	333	87	87	34	53
36	714	352	362	88	74	21	53
37	688	338	350	89	56	11	45
38	747	396	351				
39	677	346	331	90 and over	168	41	127
40-44	3345	1631	1714	Under 16	12334	6285	6049
40	675	322	353				
41	685	332	353	Under 18	14129	7205	6924
42	673	336	337				
43	664	320	344	16-44	20384	10520	9864
44	648	321	327				
45-49	3098	1605	1493	45-59/64*	8888	4994	3894
45	678	365	313				
46	634	327	307	60/65** and over	6503	2379	4124
47	594	313	281				
48	612	314	298				
49	580	286	294				

*   45 – 64 for males; 45 – 59 for females.
** 65 and over for males; 60 and over for females.

Table M2

Mid-Year Population at 30 June 2001: Resident population by single year of age and sex

Age	All Persons	Males	Females	Age	All Persons	Males	Females
All Ages ·	38273	19164	19109	50-54	2219	1116	1103
0-4	3013	1565	1448	50	445	243	202
0	554	283	271	51	455	218	237
1	548	296	252	52	437	223	214
2	607	308	299	53	419	201	218
3	633	331	302	54	463	231	232
4	671	347	324				
				55-59	1902	956	946
5-9	2914	1484	1430	55	411	214	197
5	612	317	295	56	401	201	200
6	564	284	280	57	397	206	191
7	567	295	272	58	335	161	174
8	572	285	287	59	358	174	184
9	599	303	296				
				60-64	1646	807	839
10-14	3278	1671	1607	60	332	160	172
10	609	320	289	61	341	170	171
11	649	315	334	62	324	157	167
12	637	324	313	63	332	162	170
13	667	335	332	64	317	158	159
14	716	377	339				
				65-69	1372	659	713
15-19	3180	1627	1553	65	287	148	139
15	706	366	340	66	283	136	147
16	685	363	322	67	279	130	149
17	648	337	311	68	265	118	147
18	647	313	334	69	258	127	131
19	494	248	246				
				70-74	1227	557	670
20-24	2339	1213	1126	70	258	128	130
20	440	235	205	71	245	126	119
21	466	258	208	72	258	103	155
22	462	243	219	73	238	99	139
23	492	241	251	74	228	101	127
24	479	236	243				
				75-79	880	371	509
25-29	2834	1440	1394	75	208	99	109
25	473	242	231	76	203	95	108
26	493	250	243	77	171	63	108
27	527	254	273	78	154	59	95
28	657	356	301	79	144	55	89
29	684	338	346				
				80-84	568	229	339
30-34	2945	1450	1495	80	132	57	75
30	579	264	315	81	146	60	86
31	592	276	316	82	122	48	74
32	555	271	284	83	92	36	56
33	609	322	287	84	76	28	48
34	610	317	293				
				85-89	280	95	185
35-39	2929	1521	1408	85	61	24	37
35	616	328	288	86	64	26	38
36	638	316	322	87	58	21	37
37	595	328	267	88	57	14	43
38	543	270	273	89	40	10	30
39	537	279	258				
				90 and over	118	36	82
40-44	2435	1232	1203				
40	517	287	230	Under 16	9911	5086	4825
41	490	259	231				
42	480	231	249	Under 18	11244	5786	5458
43	482	234	248				
44	466	221	245	16-44	15956	8117	7839
45-49	2194	1135	1059	45-59/64*	7122	4014	3108
45	448	225	223				
46	440	225	215	60/65** and over	5284	1947	3337
47	458	256	202				
48	443	222	221				
49	405	207	198				

* 45 – 64 for males; 45 – 59 for females.
** 65 and over for males; 60 and over for females.

MID-YEAR ESTIMATES

Table M3

Mid-Year Population at 30 June 2001: Resident population by single year of age and sex

Age	All Persons	Males	Females	Age	All Persons	Males	Females
All Ages	666860	319500	347360	50-54	38856	18925	19931
				50	7554	3755	3799
0-4	41825	21502	20323	51	7671	3746	3925
0	7870	3967	3903	52	7686	3734	3952
1	8054	4184	3870	53	7938	3847	4091
2	8391	4332	4059	54	8007	3843	4164
3	8580	4459	4121				
4	8930	4560	4370	55-59	36220	17625	18595
				55	7364	3632	3732
5-9	46261	23682	22579	56	7315	3562	3753
5	8848	4587	4261	57	7459	3582	3877
6	8947	4561	4386	58	7440	3591	3849
7	9109	4596	4513	59	6642	3258	3384
8	9443	4782	4661				
9	9914	5156	4758	60-64	29629	14065	15564
				60	5930	2856	3074
10-14	49339	25153	24186	61	5877	2801	3076
10	9857	5037	4820	62	6042	2848	3194
11	9679	4892	4787	63	5867	2778	3089
12	9837	5000	4837	64	5913	2782	3131
13	9976	5104	4872				
14	9990	5120	4870	65-69	27294	12387	14907
				65	5752	2634	3118
15-19	49656	25009	24647	66	5509	2571	2938
15	10032	5105	4927	67	5342	2468	2874
16	10092	5130	4962	68	5382	2361	3021
17	9681	4926	4755	69	5309	2353	2956
18	9622	4952	4670				
19	10229	4896	5333	70-74	24982	10533	14449
				70	5319	2309	3010
20-24	45558	22462	23096	71	5201	2181	3020
20	9940	4886	5054	72	4928	2085	2843
21	9632	4881	4751	73	4762	1994	2768
22	9052	4430	4622	74	4772	1964	2808
23	8515	4140	4375				
24	8419	4125	4294	75-79	20440	7938	12502
				75	4597	1835	2762
25-29	44413	21821	22592	76	4316	1740	2576
25	8645	4287	4358	77	4033	1566	2467
26	8554	4224	4330	78	3778	1426	2352
27	8848	4287	4561	79	3716	1371	2345
28	9235	4466	4769				
29	9131	4557	4574	80-84	13699	4889	8810
				80	3610	1354	2256
30-34	49408	23736	25672	81	3367	1267	2100
30	9610	4640	4970	82	2577	935	1642
31	9601	4617	4984	83	2154	703	1451
32	9863	4704	5159	84	1991	630	1361
33	10016	4839	5177				
34	10318	4936	5382	85-89	7397	2112	5285
				85	1823	540	1283
35-39	51313	24557	26756	86	1730	508	1222
35	10219	4955	5264	87	1500	439	1061
36	10515	5065	5450	88	1305	355	950
37	10337	4933	5404	89	1039	270	769
38	10176	4864	5312				
39	10066	4740	5326	90 and over	3521	749	2772
40-44	46923	22445	24478	Under 16	147457	75442	72015
40	9935	4742	5193				
41	9592	4632	4960	Under 18	167230	85498	81732
42	9256	4368	4888				
43	9295	4473	4822	16-44	277239	134925	142314
44	8845	4230	4615				
				45-59/64*	129267	70525	58742
45-49	40126	19910	20216				
45	8558	4224	4334	60/65** and over	112897	38608	74289
46	8018	3979	4039				
47	8029	4015	4014				
48	7901	3882	4019				
49	7620	3810	3810				

* 45 – 64 for males; 45 – 59 for females.
** 65 and over for males; 60 and over for females.

Table M3

Mid-Year Population at 30 June 2001: Resident population by single year of age and sex

Age	All Persons	Males	Females
All Ages	428226	209943	218283
0-4	28871	14912	13959
0	5397	2872	2525
1	5670	2919	2751
2	5819	2980	2839
3	5903	3024	2879
4	6082	3117	2965
5-9	30380	15535	14845
5	5934	3059	2875
6	6004	3096	2908
7	6061	3059	3002
8	6134	3133	3001
9	6247	3188	3059
10-14	32534	16679	15855
10	6367	3229	3138
11	6428	3292	3136
12	6468	3329	3139
13	6614	3390	3224
14	6657	3439	3218
15-19	31258	15856	15402
15	6662	3427	3235
16	6613	3430	3183
17	6318	3157	3161
18	6107	3069	3038
19	5558	2773	2785
20-24	26686	13358	13328
20	5515	2797	2718
21	5411	2694	2717
22	5373	2712	2661
23	5192	2554	2638
24	5195	2601	2594
25-29	28938	14375	14563
25	5282	2625	2657
26	5386	2597	2789
27	5836	2994	2842
28	6077	3031	3046
29	6357	3128	3229
30-34	33262	16551	16711
30	6676	3363	3313
31	6556	3272	3284
32	6655	3326	3329
33	6672	3267	3405
34	6703	3323	3380
35-39	33458	16521	16937
35	6743	3364	3379
36	6913	3382	3531
37	6888	3389	3499
38	6601	3320	3281
39	6313	3066	3247
40-44	30045	14879	15166
40	6245	3088	3157
41	6124	3004	3120
42	5967	3027	2940
43	5939	2914	3025
44	5770	2846	2924
45-49	26724	13562	13162
45	5639	2795	2844
46	5357	2733	2624
47	5278	2750	2528
48	5303	2686	2617
49	5147	2598	2549
50-54	25719	12743	12976
50	5150	2609	2541
51	5143	2561	2582
52	5017	2463	2554
53	5076	2499	2577
54	5333	2611	2722
55-59	23780	11691	12089
55	4885	2419	2466
56	4776	2336	2440
57	4892	2429	2463
58	4827	2395	2432
59	4400	2112	2288
60-64	19684	9422	10262
60	4022	1963	2059
61	4002	1888	2114
62	3987	1913	2074
63	3844	1847	1997
64	3829	1811	2018
65-69	16989	8069	8920
65	3610	1737	1873
66	3479	1656	1823
67	3385	1614	1771
68	3308	1555	1753
69	3207	1507	1700
70-74	14747	6537	8210
70	3239	1446	1793
71	3086	1398	1688
72	2902	1307	1595
73	2726	1165	1561
74	2794	1221	1573
75-79	11800	4878	6922
75	2660	1122	1538
76	2454	1073	1381
77	2350	993	1357
78	2206	857	1349
79	2130	833	1297
80-84	7662	2866	4796
80	1946	769	1177
81	1795	676	1119
82	1525	552	973
83	1269	461	808
84	1127	408	719
85-89	3935	1119	2816
85	968	306	662
86	904	256	648
87	817	219	598
88	684	200	484
89	562	138	424
90 and over	1754	390	1364
Under 16	98447	50553	47894
Under 18	111378	57140	54238
16-44	176985	88113	88872
45-59/64*	85645	47418	38227
60/65** and over	67149	23859	43290

*   45 – 64 for males; 45 – 59 for females.
** 65 and over for males; 60 and over for females.

MID-YEAR ESTIMATES

83

Table M3

Mid-Year Population at 30 June 2001: Resident population by single year of age and sex

Age	All Persons	Males	Females	Age	All Persons	Males	Females
All Ages	312190	154692	157498	50-54	17766	8758	9008
				50	3488	1735	1753
0-4	23050	11862	11188	51	3590	1772	1818
0	4322	2274	2048	52	3621	1822	1799
1	4565	2331	2234	53	3559	1728	1831
2	4652	2346	2306	54	3508	1701	1807
3	4745	2470	2275				
4	4766	2441	2325	55-59	15864	7851	8013
				55	3326	1635	1691
5-9	24233	12577	11656	56	3300	1635	1665
5	4728	2470	2258	57	3193	1597	1596
6	4795	2544	2251	58	3168	1561	1607
7	4800	2474	2326	59	2877	1423	1454
8	4862	2489	2373				
9	5048	2600	2448	60-64	13188	6401	6787
				60	2713	1324	1389
10-14	26203	13566	12637	61	2676	1338	1338
10	5211	2730	2481	62	2641	1262	1379
11	5154	2693	2461	63	2551	1231	1320
12	5201	2735	2466	64	2607	1246	1361
13	5280	2658	2622				
14	5357	2750	2607	65-69	11715	5498	6217
				65	2558	1244	1314
15-19	24727	12637	12090	66	2373	1130	1243
15	5271	2719	2552	67	2327	1068	1259
16	5365	2676	2689	68	2262	1030	1232
17	5238	2648	2590	69	2195	1026	1169
18	4951	2549	2402				
19	3902	2045	1857	70-74	9909	4313	5596
				70	2145	929	1216
20-24	19284	9875	9409	71	2083	931	1152
20	3671	1975	1696	72	1958	873	1085
21	3902	2036	1866	73	1912	815	1097
22	3863	1944	1919	74	1811	765	1046
23	3866	1948	1918				
24	3982	1972	2010	75-79	7930	3235	4695
				75	1785	752	1033
25-29	21184	10580	10604	76	1699	691	1008
25	3978	2011	1967	77	1579	660	919
26	3918	2015	1903	78	1499	606	893
27	4221	2105	2116	79	1368	526	842
28	4417	2223	2194				
29	4650	2226	2424	80-84	5036	1847	3189
				80	1300	477	823
30-34	23785	11959	11826	81	1171	434	737
30	4738	2384	2354	82	1019	384	635
31	4699	2392	2307	83	807	293	514
32	4728	2348	2380	84	739	259	480
33	4821	2435	2386				
34	4799	2400	2399	85-89	2609	817	1792
				85	712	240	472
35-39	24026	12098	11928	86	616	193	423
35	4837	2452	2385	87	507	159	348
36	4940	2490	2450	88	428	134	294
37	4897	2466	2431	89	346	91	255
38	4745	2386	2359				
39	4607	2304	2303	90 and over	1092	244	848
40-44	21746	10913	10833	Under 16	78757	40724	38033
40	4588	2317	2271				
41	4547	2257	2290	Under 18	89360	46048	43312
42	4231	2116	2115				
43	4253	2136	2117	16-44	129481	65343	64138
44	4127	2087	2040				
				45-59/64*	58874	32671	26203
45-49	18843	9661	9182				
45	3976	2019	1957	60/65** and over	45078	15954	29124
46	3836	2001	1835				
47	3759	1920	1839				
48	3767	1959	1808				
49	3505	1762	1743				

*   45 – 64 for males; 45 – 59 for females.
**   65 and over for males; 60 and over for females.

MID-YEAR ESTIMATES

Table M3

Mid-Year Population at 30 June 2001: Resident population by single year of age and sex

Age	All Persons	Males	Females	Age	All Persons	Males	Females
All Ages	282043	140294	141749	50-54	15896	7997	7899
				50	3252	1647	1605
0-4	21003	10799	10204	51	3238	1633	1605
0	3924	2014	1910	52	3221	1622	1599
1	4009	2077	1932	53	3046	1507	1539
2	4256	2166	2090	54	3139	1588	1551
3	4337	2219	2118				
4	4477	2323	2154	55-59	13489	6695	6794
				55	2861	1456	1405
5-9	21979	11225	10754	56	2762	1361	1401
5	4453	2314	2139	57	2814	1422	1392
6	4319	2197	2122	58	2639	1273	1366
7	4360	2240	2120	59	2413	1183	1230
8	4394	2219	2175				
9	4453	2255	2198	60-64	11218	5586	5632
				60	2312	1143	1169
10-14	24366	12493	11873	61	2239	1118	1121
10	4684	2406	2278	62	2277	1133	1144
11	4748	2414	2334	63	2206	1126	1080
12	4820	2463	2357	64	2184	1066	1118
13	5011	2586	2425				
14	5103	2624	2479	65-69	9505	4533	4972
				65	2050	981	1069
15-19	24229	12535	11694	66	1916	942	974
15	5141	2653	2488	67	1890	881	1009
16	5084	2621	2463	68	1827	856	971
17	5173	2649	2524	69	1822	873	949
18	4868	2495	2373				
19	3963	2117	1846	70-74	8214	3707	4507
				70	1732	824	908
20-24	18864	9862	9002	71	1649	770	879
20	3750	2003	1747	72	1679	718	961
21	3769	2046	1723	73	1577	678	899
22	3748	1940	1808	74	1577	717	860
23	3807	1932	1875				
24	3790	1941	1849	75-79	6480	2599	3881
				75	1466	634	832
25-29	20329	10182	10147	76	1356	563	793
25	3784	1925	1859	77	1305	522	783
26	3859	1914	1945	78	1238	463	775
27	4013	2001	2012	79	1115	417	698
28	4299	2152	2147				
29	4374	2190	2184	80-84	4140	1579	2561
				80	1035	418	617
30-34	21494	10719	10775	81	978	374	604
30	4300	2121	2179	82	856	337	519
31	4307	2125	2182	83	676	246	430
32	4308	2129	2179	84	595	204	391
33	4347	2192	2155				
34	4232	2152	2080	85-89	2215	699	1516
				85	561	192	369
35-39	21433	10735	10698	86	505	170	335
35	4371	2163	2208	87	449	141	308
36	4478	2246	2232	88	390	112	278
37	4252	2148	2104	89	310	84	226
38	4241	2121	2120				
39	4091	2057	2034	90 and over	901	234	667
40-44	19087	9405	9682	Under 16	72489	37170	35319
40	4081	2034	2047				
41	3922	1948	1974	Under 18	82746	42440	40306
42	3756	1815	1941				
43	3737	1828	1909	16-44	120295	60785	59510
44	3591	1780	1811				
				45-59/64*	52172	28988	23184
45-49	17201	8710	8491				
45	3620	1854	1766	60/65** and over	37087	13351	23736
46	3572	1847	1725				
47	3446	1748	1698				
48	3341	1674	1667				
49	3222	1587	1635				

*   45 – 64 for males; 45 – 59 for females.
** 65 and over for males; 60 and over for females.

MID-YEAR ESTIMATES

Table M4

Mid-Year Population at 30 June 2001: Resident population by single year of age and sex

Age	All Persons	Males	Females	Age	All Persons	Males	Females
All Ages	277170	129804	147366	50-54	14173	6847	7326
				50	2832	1395	1437
0-4	16499	8439	8060	51	2803	1333	1470
0	3229	1625	1604	52	2720	1323	1397
1	3136	1651	1485	53	2855	1394	1461
2	3252	1689	1563	54	2963	1402	1561
3	3328	1707	1621				
4	3554	1767	1787	55-59	13701	6546	7155
				55	2749	1340	1409
5-9	18615	9444	9171	56	2709	1303	1406
5	3415	1746	1669	57	2784	1315	1469
6	3535	1768	1767	58	2874	1357	1517
7	3724	1842	1882	59	2585	1231	1354
8	3902	1970	1932				
9	4039	2118	1921	60-64	12100	5673	6427
				60	2295	1111	1184
10-14	20525	10444	10081	61	2386	1128	1258
10	3985	2040	1945	62	2449	1129	1320
11	3921	1962	1959	63	2475	1151	1324
12	4124	2109	2015	64	2495	1154	1341
13	4251	2137	2114				
14	4244	2196	2048	65-69	11690	5141	6549
				65	2444	1069	1375
15-19	22340	10971	11369	66	2318	1024	1294
15	4307	2190	2117	67	2308	1034	1274
16	4288	2197	2091	68	2297	989	1308
17	4053	2074	1979	69	2323	1025	1298
18	4198	2128	2070				
19	5494	2382	3112	70-74	11001	4451	6550
				70	2366	957	1409
20-24	23526	11118	12408	71	2318	941	1377
20	5379	2416	2963	72	2130	873	1257
21	5099	2397	2702	73	2094	848	1246
22	4669	2229	2440	74	2093	832	1261
23	4222	2033	2189				
24	4157	2043	2114	75-79	8982	3339	5643
				75	2019	797	1222
25-29	20226	9662	10564	76	1929	756	1173
25	4209	2018	2191	77	1769	625	1144
26	4083	1959	2124	78	1650	596	1054
27	4051	1887	2164	79	1615	565	1050
28	4106	1969	2137				
29	3777	1829	1948	80-84	5891	1986	3905
				80	1572	560	1012
30-34	19564	9163	10401	81	1460	525	935
30	3941	1859	2082	82	1125	385	740
31	3897	1862	2035	83	900	268	632
32	3850	1778	2072	84	834	248	586
33	3848	1818	2030				
34	4028	1846	2182	85-89	3276	906	2370
				85	785	229	556
35-39	19857	9311	10546	86	791	236	555
35	3980	1877	2103	87	681	192	489
36	4039	1921	2118	88	566	137	429
37	4062	1921	2141	89	453	112	341
38	3902	1809	2093				
39	3874	1783	2091	90 and over	1534	300	1234
40-44	18414	8554	9860	Under 16	59946	30517	29429
40	3871	1811	2060				
41	3735	1756	1979	Under 18	68287	34788	33499
42	3641	1650	1991				
43	3647	1721	1926	16-44	119620	56589	63031
44	3520	1616	1904				
				45-59/64*	48803	26575	22228
45-49	15256	7509	7747				
45	3263	1561	1702	60/65** and over	48801	16123	32678
46	3071	1509	1562				
47	3053	1506	1547				
48	3024	1482	1542				
49	2845	1451	1394				

*   45 – 64 for males; 45 – 59 for females.
**   65 and over for males; 60 and over for females.

MID-YEAR ESTIMATES

Table M4

Mid-Year Population at 30 June 2001: Resident population by single year of age and sex

Age	All Persons	Males	Females	Age	All Persons	Males	Females
All Ages	395514	193679	201835	50-54	23863	11826	12037
				50	4763	2419	2344
0-4	26499	13668	12831	51	4778	2380	2398
0	4963	2623	2340	52	4659	2292	2367
1	5196	2682	2514	53	4704	2318	2386
2	5337	2739	2598	54	4959	2417	2542
3	5433	2772	2661				
4	5570	2852	2718	55-59	22102	10859	11243
				55	4532	2253	2279
5-9	27815	14230	13585	56	4424	2163	2261
5	5438	2788	2650	57	4543	2249	2294
6	5484	2828	2656	58	4501	2227	2274
7	5563	2808	2755	59	4102	1967	2135
8	5616	2879	2737				
9	5714	2927	2787	60-64	18355	8779	9576
				60	3734	1809	1925
10-14	29631	15195	14436	61	3714	1751	1963
10	5799	2941	2858	62	3725	1792	1933
11	5849	2994	2855	63	3590	1727	1863
12	5885	3030	2855	64	3592	1700	1892
13	6030	3092	2938				
14	6068	3138	2930	65-69	15920	7557	8363
				65	3375	1622	1753
15-19	28456	14420	14036	66	3260	1541	1719
15	6057	3108	2949	67	3170	1511	1659
16	5979	3099	2880	68	3103	1459	1644
17	5716	2860	2856	69	3012	1424	1588
18	5554	2794	2760				
19	5150	2559	2591	70-74	13776	6075	7701
				70	3052	1350	1702
20-24	24466	12185	12281	71	2873	1291	1582
20	5064	2560	2504	72	2692	1213	1479
21	4957	2461	2496	73	2552	1085	1467
22	4939	2480	2459	74	2607	1136	1471
23	4752	2323	2429				
24	4754	2361	2393	75-79	10991	4527	6464
				75	2491	1044	1447
25-29	26614	13212	13402	76	2285	995	1290
25	4801	2387	2414	77	2170	909	1261
26	4951	2386	2565	78	2067	805	1262
27	5382	2760	2622	79	1978	774	1204
28	5604	2792	2812				
29	5876	2887	2989	80-84	7128	2672	4456
				80	1811	716	1095
30-34	30929	15400	15529	81	1662	630	1032
30	6169	3108	3061	82	1415	507	908
31	6089	3031	3058	83	1189	435	754
32	6222	3115	3107	84	1051	384	667
33	6198	3037	3161				
34	6251	3109	3142	85-89	3663	1037	2626
				85	901	284	617
35-39	31074	15329	15745	86	836	238	598
35	6271	3145	3126	87	768	202	566
36	6419	3135	3284	88	627	183	444
37	6385	3134	3251	89	531	130	401
38	6127	3057	3070				
39	5872	2858	3014	90 and over	1644	357	1287
40-44	27815	13772	14043	Under 16	90002	46201	43801
40	5795	2873	2922				
41	5654	2780	2874	Under 18	101697	52160	49537
42	5537	2785	2752				
43	5501	2710	2791	16-44	163297	81210	82087
44	5328	2624	2704				
				45-59/64*	79517	44043	35474
45-49	24773	12579	12194				
45	5228	2592	2636	60/65** and over	62698	22225	40473
46	4965	2532	2433				
47	4898	2560	2338				
48	4911	2475	2436				
49	4771	2420	2351				

*   45 – 64 for males; 45 – 59 for females.
**   65 and over for males; 60 and over for females.

Table M4

Mid-Year Population at 30 June 2001: Resident population by single year of age and sex

Age	All Persons	Males	Females
All Ages	389690	189696	199994
0-4	25326	13063	12263
0	4641	2342	2299
1	4918	2533	2385
2	5139	2643	2496
3	5252	2752	2500
4	5376	2793	2583
5-9	27646	14238	13408
5	5433	2841	2592
6	5412	2793	2619
7	5385	2754	2631
8	5541	2812	2729
9	5875	3038	2837
10-14	28814	14709	14105
10	5872	2997	2875
11	5758	2930	2828
12	5713	2891	2822
13	5725	2967	2758
14	5746	2924	2822
15-19	27316	14038	13278
15	5725	2915	2810
16	5804	2933	2871
17	5628	2852	2776
18	5424	2824	2600
19	4735	2514	2221
20-24	22032	11344	10688
20	4561	2470	2091
21	4533	2484	2049
22	4383	2201	2182
23	4293	2107	2186
24	4262	2082	2180
25-29	24187	12159	12028
25	4436	2269	2167
26	4471	2265	2206
27	4797	2400	2397
28	5129	2497	2632
29	5354	2728	2626
30-34	29844	14573	15271
30	5669	2781	2888
31	5704	2755	2949
32	6013	2926	3087
33	6168	3021	3147
34	6290	3090	3200
35-39	31456	15246	16210
35	6239	3078	3161
36	6476	3144	3332
37	6275	3012	3263
38	6274	3055	3219
39	6192	2957	3235
40-44	28509	13891	14618
40	6064	2931	3133
41	5857	2876	2981
42	5615	2718	2897
43	5648	2752	2896
44	5325	2614	2711
45-49	24870	12401	12469
45	5295	2663	2632
46	4947	2470	2477
47	4976	2509	2467
48	4877	2400	2477
49	4775	2359	2416

Age	All Persons	Males	Females
50-54	24683	12078	12605
50	4722	2360	2362
51	4868	2413	2455
52	4966	2411	2555
53	5083	2453	2630
54	5044	2441	2603
55-59	22519	11079	11440
55	4615	2292	2323
56	4606	2259	2347
57	4675	2267	2408
58	4566	2234	2332
59	4057	2027	2030
60-64	17529	8392	9137
60	3635	1745	1890
61	3491	1673	1818
62	3593	1719	1874
63	3392	1627	1765
64	3418	1628	1790
65-69	15604	7246	8358
65	3308	1565	1743
66	3191	1547	1644
67	3034	1434	1600
68	3085	1372	1713
69	2986	1328	1658
70-74	13981	6082	7899
70	2953	1352	1601
71	2883	1240	1643
72	2798	1212	1586
73	2668	1146	1522
74	2679	1132	1547
75-79	11458	4599	6859
75	2578	1038	1540
76	2387	984	1403
77	2264	941	1323
78	2128	830	1298
79	2101	806	1295
80-84	7808	2903	4905
80	2038	794	1244
81	1907	742	1165
82	1452	550	902
83	1254	435	819
84	1157	382	775
85-89	4121	1206	2915
85	1038	311	727
86	939	272	667
87	819	247	572
88	739	218	521
89	586	158	428
90 and over	1987	449	1538
Under 16	87511	44925	42586
Under 18	98943	50710	48233
16-44	157619	78336	79283
45-59/64*	80464	43950	36514
60/65** and over	64096	22485	41611

* 45 – 64 for males; 45 – 59 for females.
** 65 and over for males; 60 and over for females.

MID-YEAR ESTIMATES

Table M4

Mid-Year Population at 30 June 2001: Resident population by single year of age and sex

Age	All Persons	Males	Females	Age	All Persons	Males	Females
All Ages	344902	170956	173946	50-54	19622	9675	9947
				50	3875	1925	1950
0-4	25422	13106	12316	51	3955	1953	2002
0	4756	2523	2233	52	3979	1993	1986
1	5039	2568	2471	53	3931	1909	2022
2	5134	2587	2547	54	3882	1895	1987
3	5215	2722	2493				
4	5278	2706	2572	55-59	17542	8683	8859
				55	3679	1801	1878
5-9	26798	13882	12916	56	3652	1808	1844
5	5224	2741	2483	57	3542	1777	1765
6	5315	2812	2503	58	3494	1729	1765
7	5298	2725	2573	59	3175	1568	1607
8	5380	2743	2637				
9	5581	2861	2720	60-64	14517	7044	7473
				60	3001	1478	1523
10-14	29106	15050	14056	61	2964	1475	1489
10	5779	3018	2761	62	2903	1383	1520
11	5733	2991	2742	63	2805	1351	1454
12	5784	3034	2750	64	2844	1357	1487
13	5864	2956	2908				
14	5946	3051	2895	65-69	12784	6010	6774
				65	2793	1359	1434
15-19	27529	14073	13456	66	2592	1245	1347
15	5876	3038	2838	67	2542	1171	1371
16	5999	3007	2992	68	2467	1126	1341
17	5840	2945	2895	69	2390	1109	1281
18	5504	2824	2680				
19	4310	2259	2051	70-74	10880	4775	6105
				70	2332	1025	1307
20-24	21504	11048	10456	71	2296	1038	1258
20	4122	2212	1910	72	2168	967	1201
21	4356	2269	2087	73	2086	895	1191
22	4297	2176	2121	74	1998	850	1148
23	4306	2179	2127				
24	4423	2212	2211	75-79	8739	3586	5153
				75	1954	830	1124
25-29	23508	11743	11765	76	1868	769	1099
25	4459	2249	2210	77	1759	744	1015
26	4353	2226	2127	78	1638	658	980
27	4675	2339	2336	79	1520	585	935
28	4890	2462	2428				
29	5131	2467	2664	80-84	5570	2041	3529
				80	1435	530	905
30-34	26118	13110	13008	81	1304	480	824
30	5245	2639	2606	82	1129	429	700
31	5166	2633	2533	83	887	319	568
32	5161	2559	2602	84	815	283	532
33	5295	2665	2630				
34	5251	2614	2637	85-89	2881	899	1982
				85	779	262	517
35-39	26410	13290	13120	86	684	211	473
35	5309	2671	2638	87	556	176	380
36	5434	2737	2697	88	485	151	334
37	5400	2721	2679	89	377	99	278
38	5219	2649	2570				
39	5048	2512	2536	90 and over	1202	277	925
40-44	23976	12020	11956	Under 16	87202	45076	42126
40	5038	2532	2506				
41	5017	2481	2536	Under 18	99041	51028	48013
42	4661	2358	2303				
43	4691	2340	2351	16-44	143169	72246	70923
44	4569	2309	2260				
				45-59/64*	65002	36046	28956
45-49	20794	10644	10150				
45	4387	2222	2165	60/65** and over	49529	17588	31941
46	4228	2202	2026				
47	4139	2110	2029				
48	4159	2170	1989				
49	3881	1940	1941				

*   45 – 64 for males; 45 – 59 for females.
** 65 and over for males; 60 and over for females.

Table M4

Mid-Year Population at 30 June 2001: Resident population by single year of age and sex

Age	All Persons	Males	Females	Age	All Persons	Males	Females
All Ages	282043	140294	141749	50-54	15896	7997	7899
				50	3252	1647	1605
0-4	21003	10799	10204	51	3238	1633	1605
0	3924	2014	1910	52	3221	1622	1599
1	4009	2077	1932	53	3046	1507	1539
2	4256	2166	2090	54	3139	1588	1551
3	4337	2219	2118				
4	4477	2323	2154	55-59	13489	6695	6794
				55	2861	1456	1405
5-9	21979	11225	10754	56	2762	1361	1401
5	4453	2314	2139	57	2814	1422	1392
6	4319	2197	2122	58	2639	1273	1366
7	4360	2240	2120	59	2413	1183	1230
8	4394	2219	2175				
9	4453	2255	2198	60-64	11218	5586	5632
				60	2312	1143	1169
10-14	24366	12493	11873	61	2239	1118	1121
10	4684	2406	2278	62	2277	1133	1144
11	4748	2414	2334	63	2206	1126	1080
12	4820	2463	2357	64	2184	1066	1118
13	5011	2586	2425				
14	5103	2624	2479	65-69	9505	4533	4972
				65	2050	981	1069
15-19	24229	12535	11694	66	1916	942	974
15	5141	2653	2488	67	1890	881	1009
16	5084	2621	2463	68	1827	856	971
17	5173	2649	2524	69	1822	873	949
18	4868	2495	2373				
19	3963	2117	1846	70-74	8214	3707	4507
				70	1732	824	908
20-24	18864	9862	9002	71	1649	770	879
20	3750	2003	1747	72	1679	718	961
21	3769	2046	1723	73	1577	678	899
22	3748	1940	1808	74	1577	717	860
23	3807	1932	1875				
24	3790	1941	1849	75-79	6480	2599	3881
				75	1466	634	832
25-29	20329	10182	10147	76	1356	563	793
25	3784	1925	1859	77	1305	522	783
26	3859	1914	1945	78	1238	463	775
27	4013	2001	2012	79	1115	417	698
28	4299	2152	2147				
29	4374	2190	2184	80-84	4140	1579	2561
				80	1035	418	617
30-34	21494	10719	10775	81	978	374	604
30	4300	2121	2179	82	856	337	519
31	4307	2125	2182	83	676	246	430
32	4308	2129	2179	84	595	204	391
33	4347	2192	2155				
34	4232	2152	2080	85-89	2215	699	1516
				85	561	192	369
35-39	21433	10735	10698	86	505	170	335
35	4371	2163	2208	87	449	141	308
36	4478	2246	2232	88	390	112	278
37	4252	2148	2104	89	310	84	226
38	4241	2121	2120				
39	4091	2057	2034	90 and over	901	234	667
40-44	19087	9405	9682	Under 16	72489	37170	35319
40	4081	2034	2047				
41	3922	1948	1974	Under 18	82746	42440	40306
42	3756	1815	1941				
43	3737	1828	1909	16-44	120295	60785	59510
44	3591	1780	1811				
				45-59/64*	52172	28988	23184
45-49	17201	8710	8491				
45	3620	1854	1766	60/65** and over	37087	13351	23736
46	3572	1847	1725				
47	3446	1748	1698				
48	3341	1674	1667				
49	3222	1587	1635				

* 45 – 64 for males; 45 – 59 for females.
** 65 and over for males; 60 and over for females.

MID-YEAR ESTIMATES

Table M5

Mid-Year Population at 30 June 2001: Resident population by single year of age and sex

Age	All Persons	Males	Females	Age	All Persons	Males	Females
All Ages	277170	129804	147366	50-54	14173	6847	7326
				50	2832	1395	1437
0-4	16499	8439	8060	51	2803	1333	1470
0	3229	1625	1604	52	2720	1323	1397
1	3136	1651	1485	53	2855	1394	1461
2	3252	1689	1563	54	2963	1402	1561
3	3328	1707	1621				
4	3554	1767	1787	55-59	13701	6546	7155
				55	2749	1340	1409
5-9	18615	9444	9171	56	2709	1303	1406
5	3415	1746	1669	57	2784	1315	1469
6	3535	1768	1767	58	2874	1357	1517
7	3724	1842	1882	59	2585	1231	1354
8	3902	1970	1932				
9	4039	2118	1921	60-64	12100	5673	6427
				60	2295	1111	1184
10-14	20525	10444	10081	61	2386	1128	1258
10	3985	2040	1945	62	2449	1129	1320
11	3921	1962	1959	63	2475	1151	1324
12	4124	2109	2015	64	2495	1154	1341
13	4251	2137	2114				
14	4244	2196	2048	65-69	11690	5141	6549
				65	2444	1069	1375
15-19	22340	10971	11369	66	2318	1024	1294
15	4307	2190	2117	67	2308	1034	1274
16	4288	2197	2091	68	2297	989	1308
17	4053	2074	1979	69	2323	1025	1298
18	4198	2128	2070				
19	5494	2382	3112	70-74	11001	4451	6550
				70	2366	957	1409
20-24	23526	11118	12408	71	2318	941	1377
20	5379	2416	2963	72	2130	873	1257
21	5099	2397	2702	73	2094	848	1246
22	4669	2229	2440	74	2093	832	1261
23	4222	2033	2189				
24	4157	2043	2114	75-79	8982	3339	5643
				75	2019	797	1222
25-29	20226	9662	10564	76	1929	756	1173
25	4209	2018	2191	77	1769	625	1144
26	4083	1959	2124	78	1650	596	1054
27	4051	1887	2164	79	1615	565	1050
28	4106	1969	2137				
29	3777	1829	1948	80-84	5891	1986	3905
				80	1572	560	1012
30-34	19564	9163	10401	81	1460	525	935
30	3941	1859	2082	82	1125	385	740
31	3897	1862	2035	83	900	268	632
32	3850	1778	2072	84	834	248	586
33	3848	1818	2030				
34	4028	1846	2182	85-89	3276	906	2370
				85	785	229	556
35-39	19857	9311	10546	86	791	236	555
35	3980	1877	2103	87	681	192	489
36	4039	1921	2118	88	566	137	429
37	4062	1921	2141	89	453	112	341
38	3902	1809	2093				
39	3874	1783	2091	90 and over	1534	300	1234
40-44	18414	8554	9860	Under 16	59946	30517	29429
40	3871	1811	2060				
41	3735	1756	1979	Under 18	68287	34788	33499
42	3641	1650	1991				
43	3647	1721	1926	16-44	119620	56589	63031
44	3520	1616	1904				
				45-59/64*	48803	26575	22228
45-49	15256	7509	7747				
45	3263	1561	1702	60/65** and over	48801	16123	32678
46	3071	1509	1562				
47	3053	1506	1547				
48	3024	1482	1542				
49	2845	1451	1394				

*   45 – 64 for males; 45 – 59 for females.
**   65 and over for males; 60 and over for females.

MID-YEAR ESTIMATES

Table M5

Mid-Year Population at 30 June 2001: Resident population by single year of age and sex

Age	All Persons	Males	Females	Age	All Persons	Males	Females
All Ages	369982	179075	190907	50-54	22726	11041	11685
				50	4438	2214	2224
0-4	23773	12324	11449	51	4440	2222	2218
0	4396	2287	2109	52	4549	2190	2359
1	4600	2359	2241	53	4592	2185	2407
2	4778	2440	2338	54	4707	2230	2477
3	4917	2561	2356				
4	5082	2677	2405	55-59	21009	10219	10790
				55	4238	2087	2151
5-9	25987	13445	12542	56	4278	2069	2209
5	5068	2653	2415	57	4425	2118	2307
6	5124	2667	2457	58	4261	2087	2174
7	5102	2617	2485	59	3807	1858	1949
8	5189	2652	2537				
9	5504	2856	2648	60-64	16773	7992	8781
				60	3420	1669	1751
10-14	26799	13609	13190	61	3339	1577	1762
10	5482	2762	2720	62	3442	1633	1809
11	5347	2729	2618	63	3274	1564	1710
12	5301	2656	2645	64	3298	1549	1749
13	5320	2736	2584				
14	5349	2726	2623	65-69	15223	7037	8186
				65	3235	1519	1716
15-19	25360	12925	12435	66	3077	1465	1612
15	5339	2717	2622	67	2974	1374	1600
16	5344	2700	2644	68	2961	1342	1619
17	5138	2567	2571	69	2976	1337	1639
18	4900	2550	2350				
19	4639	2391	2248	70-74	13803	6028	7775
				70	2954	1344	1610
20-24	21225	10718	10507	71	2822	1230	1592
20	4398	2349	2049	72	2759	1198	1561
21	4337	2326	2011	73	2615	1111	1504
22	4198	2094	2104	74	2653	1145	1508
23	4126	1973	2153				
24	4166	1976	2190	75-79	11106	4435	6671
				75	2518	1020	1498
25-29	23470	11599	11871	76	2301	955	1346
25	4182	2078	2104	77	2215	906	1309
26	4423	2176	2247	78	2060	790	1270
27	4662	2306	2356	79	2012	764	1248
28	5006	2463	2543				
29	5197	2576	2621	80-84	7150	2597	4553
				80	1910	723	1187
30-34	28809	13958	14851	81	1749	674	1075
30	5515	2698	2817	82	1344	503	841
31	5594	2704	2890	83	1111	359	752
32	5779	2786	2993	84	1036	338	698
33	5843	2825	3018				
34	6078	2945	3133	85-89	3752	1064	2688
				85	978	278	700
35-39	30353	14710	15643	86	839	243	596
35	6005	2963	3042	87	744	208	536
36	6219	2998	3221	88	661	195	466
37	6153	2949	3204	89	530	140	390
38	6074	2952	3122				
39	5902	2848	3054	90 and over	1792	369	1423
40-44	27301	13187	14114	Under 16	81898	42095	39803
40	5846	2792	3054				
41	5577	2689	2888	Under 18	92380	47362	45018
42	5388	2604	2784				
43	5393	2640	2753	16-44	151179	74380	76799
44	5097	2462	2635				
				45-59/64*	75298	41070	34228
45-49	23571	11818	11753				
45	5030	2510	2520	60/65** and over	61607	21530	40077
46	4665	2344	2321				
47	4696	2396	2300				
48	4659	2289	2370				
49	4521	2279	2242				

* 45 – 64 for males; 45 – 59 for females.
** 65 and over for males; 60 and over for females.

MID-YEAR ESTIMATES

Table M5

Mid-Year Population at 30 June 2001: Resident population by single year of age and sex

Age	All Persons	Males	Females	Age	All Persons	Males	Females
All Ages	398435	196764	201671	50-54	24787	12250	12537
				50	4794	2420	2374
0-4	26979	13943	13036	51	4996	2457	2539
0	5100	2644	2456	52	4903	2455	2448
1	5274	2770	2504	53	5034	2454	2580
2	5432	2817	2615	54	5060	2464	2596
3	5522	2843	2679				
4	5651	2869	2782	55-59	22758	11294	11464
				55	4736	2333	2403
5-9	28810	14851	13959	56	4603	2301	2302
5	5616	2894	2722	57	4590	2304	2286
6	5639	2939	2700	58	4666	2304	2362
7	5746	2950	2796	59	4163	2052	2111
8	5843	2976	2867				
9	5966	3092	2874	60-64	18061	8688	9373
				60	3737	1808	1929
10-14	30390	15767	14623	61	3598	1719	1879
10	6015	3180	2835	62	3667	1772	1895
11	5967	3095	2872	63	3540	1704	1836
12	6026	3148	2878	64	3519	1685	1834
13	6249	3192	3057				
14	6133	3152	2981	65-69	15548	7336	8212
				65	3322	1614	1708
15-19	28860	14837	14023	66	3226	1537	1689
15	6127	3168	2959	67	3074	1452	1622
16	6171	3120	3051	68	3050	1394	1656
17	5962	3048	2914	69	2876	1339	1537
18	5785	2968	2817				
19	4815	2533	2282	70-74	13203	5845	7358
				70	2882	1298	1584
20-24	23222	11874	11348	71	2749	1222	1527
20	4705	2524	2181	72	2616	1177	1439
21	4735	2456	2279	73	2487	1093	1394
22	4652	2343	2309	74	2469	1055	1414
23	4582	2298	2284				
24	4548	2253	2295	75-79	10604	4311	6293
				75	2373	984	1389
25-29	26084	13257	12827	76	2241	939	1302
25	4806	2444	2362	77	2085	884	1201
26	4826	2432	2394	78	2002	783	1219
27	5193	2655	2538	79	1903	721	1182
28	5460	2778	2682				
29	5799	2948	2851	80-84	7236	2743	4493
				80	1836	734	1102
30-34	31382	15759	15623	81	1702	645	1057
30	6043	3011	3032	82	1443	528	915
31	6106	3073	3033	83	1198	447	751
32	6358	3231	3127	84	1057	389	668
33	6411	3199	3212				
34	6464	3245	3219	85-89	3800	1136	2664
				85	951	320	631
35-39	31789	15783	16006	86	892	256	636
35	6425	3234	3191	87	760	229	531
36	6607	3261	3346	88	654	197	457
37	6388	3168	3220	89	543	134	409
38	6303	3162	3141				
39	6066	2958	3108	90 and over	1765	401	1364
40-44	28161	14066	14095	Under 16	92306	47729	44577
40	5811	2920	2891				
41	5843	2927	2916	Under 18	104439	53897	50542
42	5599	2792	2807				
43	5610	2778	2832	16-44	163371	82408	80963
44	5298	2649	2649				
				45-59/64*	81229	44855	36374
45-49	24996	12623	12373				
45	5272	2650	2622	60/65** and over	61529	21772	39757
46	5066	2601	2465				
47	4921	2509	2412				
48	4959	2493	2466	* 45 – 64 for males; 45 – 59 for females.			
49	4778	2370	2408	** 65 and over for males; 60 and over for females.			

MID-YEAR ESTIMATES

Table M5

Mid-Year Population at 30 June 2001: Resident population by single year of age and sex

Age	All Persons	Males	Females	Age	All Persons	Males	Females
All Ages	275623	135385	140238	50-54	15592	7816	7776
				50	3152	1595	1557
0-4	20273	10453	9820	51	3188	1597	1591
0	3720	1912	1808	52	3100	1569	1531
1	3861	2028	1833	53	3022	1486	1536
2	4131	2116	2015	54	3130	1569	1561
3	4191	2132	2059				
4	4370	2265	2105	55-59	13767	6763	7004
				55	2863	1443	1420
5-9	20836	10574	10262	56	2785	1354	1431
5	4187	2164	2023	57	2877	1429	1448
6	4109	2080	2029	58	2745	1316	1429
7	4056	2045	2011	59	2497	1221	1276
8	4213	2125	2088				
9	4271	2160	2111	60-64	11765	5708	6057
				60	2433	1178	1255
10-14	23139	11840	11299	61	2334	1146	1188
10	4494	2271	2223	62	2359	1138	1221
11	4527	2311	2216	63	2330	1151	1179
12	4562	2340	2222	64	2309	1095	1214
13	4719	2408	2311				
14	4837	2510	2327	65-69	9726	4592	5134
				65	2100	1002	1098
15-19	22674	11673	11001	66	1977	953	1024
15	4772	2518	2254	67	1896	880	1016
16	4726	2471	2255	68	1900	887	1013
17	4656	2388	2268	69	1853	870	983
18	4458	2253	2205				
19	4062	2043	2019	70-74	8372	3691	4681
				70	1835	840	995
20-24	18802	9366	9436	71	1728	791	937
20	3941	1945	1996	72	1696	723	973
21	3927	1990	1937	73	1569	661	908
22	3690	1821	1869	74	1544	676	868
23	3604	1744	1860				
24	3640	1866	1774	75-79	6581	2647	3934
				75	1529	640	889
25-29	19404	9514	9890	76	1377	577	800
25	3619	1793	1826	77	1308	528	780
26	3604	1748	1856	78	1209	462	747
27	3813	1865	1948	79	1158	440	718
28	4113	2021	2092				
29	4255	2087	2168	80-84	4218	1578	2640
				80	1062	411	651
30-34	21162	10453	10709	81	992	379	613
30	4222	2077	2145	82	850	319	531
31	4144	2032	2112	83	707	256	451
32	4217	2089	2128	84	607	213	394
33	4320	2142	2178				
34	4259	2113	2146	85-89	2149	625	1524
				85	521	171	350
35-39	21170	10413	10757	86	481	158	323
35	4367	2142	2225	87	460	124	336
36	4444	2176	2268	88	388	98	290
37	4222	2122	2100	89	299	74	225
38	4064	1986	2078				
39	4073	1987	2086	90 and over	884	207	677
40-44	18648	9209	9439	Under 16	69020	35385	33635
40	4014	2025	1989				
41	3828	1909	1919	Under 18	78402	40244	38158
42	3685	1805	1880				
43	3579	1739	1840	16-44	117088	58110	58978
44	3542	1731	1811				
				45-59/64*	51528	28550	22978
45-49	16461	8263	8198				
45	3452	1704	1748	60/65** and over	37987	13340	24647
46	3396	1750	1646				
47	3327	1683	1644				
48	3212	1624	1588	* 45 – 64 for males; 45 – 59 for females.			
49	3074	1502	1572	** 65 and over for males; 60 and over for females.			

Table M5

Mid-Year Population at 30 June 2001: Resident population by single year of age and sex

Age	All Persons	Males	Females	Age	All Persons	Males	Females
All Ages	368109	183401	184708	50-54	20959	10469	10490
				50	4228	2122	2106
0-4	27225	13916	13309	51	4215	2103	2112
0	5068	2659	2409	52	4273	2104	2169
1	5427	2703	2724	53	4116	2062	2054
2	5525	2762	2763	54	4127	2078	2049
3	5607	2929	2678				
4	5598	2863	2735	55-59	18118	9040	9078
				55	3850	1939	1911
5-9	28605	14705	13900	56	3778	1867	1911
5	5677	2973	2704	57	3682	1864	1818
6	5658	2944	2714	58	3528	1756	1772
7	5702	2915	2787	59	3280	1614	1666
8	5686	2900	2786				
9	5882	2973	2909	60-64	15020	7413	7607
				60	3092	1520	1572
10-14	31589	16231	15358	61	3137	1575	1562
10	6143	3149	2994	62	3030	1484	1546
11	6247	3194	3053	63	2849	1412	1437
12	6313	3274	3039	64	2912	1422	1490
13	6342	3265	3077				
14	6544	3349	3195	65-69	13316	6381	6935
				65	2869	1392	1477
15-19	30636	15631	15005	66	2679	1320	1359
15	6561	3311	3250	67	2692	1291	1401
16	6625	3369	3256	68	2571	1190	1381
17	6601	3303	3298	69	2505	1188	1317
18	6207	3166	3041				
19	4642	2482	2160	70-74	11473	5075	6398
				70	2398	1069	1329
20-24	23617	12481	11136	71	2402	1096	1306
20	4453	2427	2026	72	2266	1012	1254
21	4616	2488	2128	73	2212	939	1273
22	4827	2539	2288	74	2195	959	1236
23	4846	2526	2320				
24	4875	2501	2374	75-79	9377	3918	5459
				75	2069	902	1167
25-29	25680	12926	12754	76	1977	840	1137
25	4873	2515	2358	77	1890	798	1092
26	4781	2435	2346	78	1800	721	1079
27	5199	2674	2525	79	1641	657	984
28	5343	2641	2702				
29	5484	2661	2823	80-84	6042	2277	3765
				80	1511	590	921
30-34	27032	13632	13400	81	1408	528	880
30	5603	2863	2740	82	1215	473	742
31	5422	2735	2687	83	990	373	617
32	5350	2623	2727	84	918	313	605
33	5434	2749	2685				
34	5223	2662	2561	85-89	3179	1016	2163
				85	829	280	549
35-39	27061	13694	13367	86	752	234	518
35	5393	2718	2675	87	628	205	423
36	5537	2827	2710	88	538	174	364
37	5549	2776	2773	89	432	123	309
38	5420	2782	2638				
39	5162	2591	2571	90 and over	1293	340	953
40-44	25277	12626	12651	Under 16	93980	48163	45817
40	5307	2633	2674				
41	5202	2560	2642	Under 18	107206	54835	52371
42	4897	2475	2422				
43	4995	2473	2522	16-44	152742	77679	75063
44	4876	2485	2391				
45-49	22610	11630	10980	45-59/64*	69100	38552	30548
45	4776	2467	2309				
46	4585	2356	2229	60/65** and over	52287	19007	33280
47	4515	2339	2176				
48	4458	2313	2145	* 45 – 64 for males; 45 – 59 for females.			
49	4276	2155	2121	** 65 and over for males; 60 and over for females.			

MID-YEAR ESTIMATES

Table M6

Mid-Year Population, at 30 June 1991 and 2001, of each Local Government District, Health and Social Services Board, Education and Library Board and NUTS Level III area, percentage change between 1991 and 2001.

| | 1991 | | | 2001 | | | Percentage change in Population |
	All Persons	Males	Females	All Persons	Males	Females	1991-2001
Northern Ireland	1607295	783150	824145	1689319	824429	864890	5.1
Local Government Districts							
Antrim	45630	22967	22663	48761	24590	24171	6.9
Ards	65259	31682	33577	73435	35836	37599	12.5
Armagh	52260	26123	26137	54462	27041	27421	4.2
Ballymena	56685	27802	28883	58801	28668	30133	3.7
Ballymoney	24232	12018	12214	27007	13349	13658	11.5
Banbridge[1]	35887	17713	18174	41549	20803	20746	15.8
Belfast	292938	137309	155629	277170	129804	147366	-5.4
Carrickfergus	33165	16018	17147	37730	18301	19429	13.8
Castlereagh	61496	29208	32288	66533	31701	34832	8.2
Coleraine	52577	25165	27412	56408	26978	29430	7.3
Cookstown	31169	15516	15653	32712	16264	16448	5.0
Craigavon	75435	36637	38798	80931	39905	41026	7.3
Derry	97597	47721	49876	105335	51355	53980	7.9
Down	58629	29170	29459	64147	31844	32303	9.4
Dungannon	45480	22568	22912	47849	23685	24164	5.2
Fermanagh	54645	27642	27003	57687	28899	28788	5.6
Larne	29624	14379	15245	30811	15118	15693	4.0
Limavady	29606	15006	14600	32639	16698	15941	10.2
Lisburn	100977	49377	51600	108997	53235	55762	7.9
Magherafelt	36366	18207	18159	39891	20076	19815	9.7
Moyle	14851	7383	7468	15961	7841	8120	7.5
Newry and Mourne[1]	81293	40555	40738	87399	43258	44141	7.5
Newtownabbey	76099	36613	39486	80144	38758	41386	5.3
North Down	73298	35185	38113	76578	37080	39498	4.5
Omagh	45933	23129	22804	48109	24178	23931	4.7
Strabane	36164	18057	18107	38273	19164	19109	5.8
Health and Social Services Boards							
Northern	400398	196068	204330	428226	209943	218283	7.0
Southern	290355	143596	146759	312190	154692	157498	7.5
Eastern	652597	311931	340666	666860	319500	347360	2.2
Western	263945	131555	132390	282043	140294	141749	6.9
Education and Library Boards							
Belfast	292938	137309	155629	277170	129804	147366	-5.4
North East	369229	180552	188677	395514	193679	201835	7.1
South East	359659	174622	185037	389690	189696	199994	8.3
Southern	321524	159112	162412	344902	170956	173946	7.3
Western	263945	131555	132390	282043	140294	141749	6.9
NUTS Level III Areas							
Belfast	292938	137309	155629	277170	129804	147366	-5.4
Outer Belfast	345035	166401	178634	369982	179075	190907	7.2
East of N.I.	367149	180350	186799	398435	196764	201671	8.5
North of N.I.	255027	125350	129677	275623	135385	140238	8.1
West and South of N.I.	347146	173740	173406	368109	183401	184708	6.0

1 All population figures in this table relate to the current Local Government District boundaries. In particular, the 1991 figures for Banbridge and Newry and Mourne have been adjusted to take account of the Local Government District boundary change of 1992 which, in effect, moved the ward of Rathfriland from Newry and Mourne Local Government District to Banbridge Local Government District.

Maps

Northern Ireland: Local Government Districts

1. Carrickfergus 4. North Down
2. Newtownabbey 5. Castlereagh
3. Belfast 6. Ards

Northern Ireland: Health and Social Services Boards

Northern Ireland: Education and Library Boards

Northern Ireland: NUTS Level III Areas

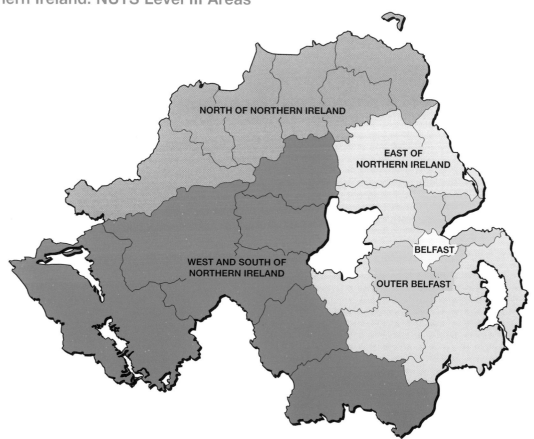